# 111 Places
# in Singapore
# That You
# Shouldn't Miss

D1550764

emons:

For Sarah, who is exploring her world here,
and our parents, who gave us free rein

© Emons Verlag GmbH
All rights reserved
Photographs by Christoph Hein, Sarah Hein
© Cover motif: shutterstock.com/Kinsei
Layout: Eva Kraskes, based on a design
by Lübbeke | Naumann | Thoben
Edited by Alison Lester
Translation by Tom Ashforth
Maps: altancicek.design, www.altancicek.de
Basic cartographical information from Openstreetmap,
© OpenStreetMap-Mitwirkende, ODbL
Printing and binding: Lensing Druck GmbH & Co. KG,
Feldbachacker 16, 44149 Dortmund
Printed in Germany 2018
ISBN 978-3-7408-0382-7
First edition

Did you enjoy it? Do you want more?
Join us in uncovering new places around the world on:
www.111places.com

# Foreword

Yes, we know all of the prejudices. Singapore, the test tube of the tropics. Asia light. A city for beginners, softies and anyone who is afraid of real life and real travel in the Asian jungle. A laboratory city, air-conditioned, guided and directed, boring and what's more, a 'fine city', a city of penalties, where chewing gum is banned.

Enough of all that. Singapore is a metropolis that can be proud of what it has to offer. A cosmopolitan city that has plenty to teach us and is prepared to be learnt from. Not everything here actually meets our expectations, but there are many things worth thinking about.

The city was and is a melting pot. A place for immigrants and millionaires, settled by seafaring nomads, built by Chinese coolies and Indian prisoners, governed by the British and persecuted by the Japanese in World War II. This hotbed of vice became a world city. The Nobel-prizewinner-in-waiting Einstein looked for money here, the Chinese revolutionary Sun Yat Sen looked for followers and the young photographer Helmut Newton for romance.

The city with its population of almost 6 million is a unique melange of newcomers, transients and the descendants of earlier immigrants. They have all brought their cultures with them. Where else in the world do churches, mosques and Hindu temples exist so peacefully side by side? Where else can you find a Chinese takeaway with Michelin stars? Where else is there a cemetery for Japanese prostitutes? And huge dunes behind barbed wire in the middle of the city?

Singapore is one of the greenest cities in the world. It is currently reinventing itself with fantastic museums and structures by the best architects in the world. At the same time it has – unlike Hong Kong – learned to respect the old.

No longer merely a red dot on the map, Singapore has long since become a leading Asian player. Its secrets are hidden, but not lost. Come with us on a journey to uncover them!

# 111 Places

# 1 ABM Salesroom

*Dream cars in a car tower*

It must be a tower – after all, anyone can spread out horizontally. This was the reasoning when the car dealership ABM decided to treat its luxury vehicles to their own tower. And now there it stands, 15 storeys high, and – just like the bubble gum machines of the past – filled with everything that is out of reach. ABM tempts its customers with Rolls-Royces and Bentleys, Aston Martins and Porsches, Ferraris, Lamborghinis and Maseratis. Models whose prices in Singapore, with its horrendous luxury tax and MOT approval fee, soon run into the millions.

While the customer watches the video of their dream car in the salesroom, it is busy making its way down to them by lift: within two minutes, the heavy-duty lift brings the car requested for viewing to the showroom at the push of a button. It doesn't come as any surprise when ABM boss Gary Hong explains that the idea for his tower came to him in a toy shop. However, he had only to visit Stevens Road in his home city, where a private house brings its residents' sports cars into their living rooms (see ch. 86), to see the principle in action. The car towers in Wolfsburg for Volkswagen and at Mercedes for its Smart cars are smaller and not to be operated by the end user. This is why Hong talks proudly of this being the 'biggest car-selling machine in the world'. The technology could also be employed for car parks in crowded city centres. The car tower on the island cost around three million Singapore dollars – so, not very much more than some of the cars themselves.

Hong runs ABM together with his three brothers. Originally they operated a rather grubby showroom on Bukit Timah Road – but this never stopped the solvent customers from visiting. The Hongs knew what they were doing. They have sold used luxury cars in the millionaire's metropolis for more than 25 years. And chose a catchy company name to do so: the abbreviation ABM stands for Autobahn Motors.

Address 20 Jalan Kilang, Suite 02-00, Singapore 159418 (Queenstown) | Getting there MRT to NS22 Orchard, then bus 123 to Opposite Block 28 on Jalan Bukit Merah | Hours Mon–Sat 9.30am–6.30pm, Sun 10.30am–6.30pm | Tip The Queensway Shopping Centre on the corner of Alexandra Road and Queensway is full of small shops that offer, in particular, branded sports shoes and glasses at very cheap prices.

# 2 The Armenian Church
*Masterpiece with national flower*

At the foot of Fort Canning Park, in the middle of the Colonial District on Hill Street, is a hidden jewel. This is the white church of Singapore's formerly influential Armenian congregation. In the 19th century it included notable businesspeople, such as the Sarkies brothers, who built the Raffles Hotel not far from here. This made it possible for them to afford to employ a distinguished city architect for the building of their church.

The Irish architect George Coleman had already created many prestigious colonial buildings in Singapore, but this one is considered his masterpiece. Based in its form on an old Armenian cross, the small church seamlessly connects elements of Western and Eastern styles. It is the oldest Christian house of worship still standing in Singapore and a national monument. But it is not these titles that make the place appealing. It is the plain beauty and the great peace that you will find here, completely unexpected in the middle of the touristic hustle and bustle. Stepping out of the silence of the white, unadorned interior of the church, you will be surprised once again by the quiet garden behind it.

Here your gaze will fall upon a large lawn with gravestones erected along its edges. But this is not a cemetery: the old inscriptions refer to members of the Armenian congregation who are buried elsewhere. Among them is the memorial stone for Agnes Joaquim, who was to play a very special role in Singapore's history: Agnes was the daughter of an Armenian businessman and, like her mother before her, a passionate gardener. In 1890 she bred the orchid called Vanda Miss Joaquim. It was so popular that it became Singapore's national flower 90 years later.

Vanda Miss Joaquim sways in the breeze next to Agnes' gravestone and seems to gently greet the visitor. And by now you should sense the trace of history at this enchanting place.

In loving memory of
AGNES.
Eldest daughter of the late
PARSICK JOAQUIM.

BORN 7TH APRIL 1854,
DIED 2ND JULY 1899.

"Let her own works praise her"

Nothing in my hand I bring
Simply to Thy cross I cling.

ԱՍ ՋԻՇԱՏԱԿԻ ՊԵՐՈՑ

AGNES JOAQUIM
AFTER WHOM THE NATIONAL
FLOWER OF SINGAPORE
THE VANDA MISS JOAQUIM
ORCHID. WAS NAMED

# 3 Artillery Shell Casing
*Singapore's head gardener*

Artillery shell casings are an abominable testimony to human slaughter. But what about when they are engraved and stand in Singapore's Botanic Gardens? This one, exhibited in a showcase in the Singapore Botanic Gardens' Heritage Museum, comes with a letter from the prime minister, Lee Hsien Loong. In it he wrote that, at the state funeral of his father, Lee Kuan Yew, four howitzers of the 21st battalion fired 21 shots in honour of the esteemed politician. One of the shiny golden shell casings was donated.

But why the Botanic Gardens of all places? Because it commemorates the greatest supporter of green Singapore. 'Mr Lee had the vision of a garden city, in which trees line the pavements and streets in order to protect the people and cool the environment, and in which land is retained for parks and green areas, so that everyone can enjoy the beauty of nature,' the son described in the letter.

The founder of the country, Lee Kuan Yew developed the concept of a green city in 1963, which was then enlarged to 'Garden City' and later to 'City in a Garden'. The greenery was intended to make the island attractive to tourists and investors. In a brochure written in the four national languages, the Botanic Gardens described how a tree is grown. The workers and researchers in the gardens helped to provide the saplings and also to increase the plant species and colours through breeding. And the citizens? They obeyed as always: they planted thousands of trees in the first year of the campaign alone. Since 1971 the city has even celebrated Tree Planting Day every November.

Lee Kuan Yew, who built up the city state with an iron fist, has long been revered as 'Singapore's head gardener'. With so much love for plants, there is a strong case for using the embellished artillery shell casing as a flower pot. The unpretentious Lee would surely have liked that.

In Memory of

MR LEE KUAN YEW
1923 – 2015

This shell was fired as part of the 21-Gun Salute
on the
Twenty-Ninth day of March
in the year
Two Thousand and Fifteen
during the State Funeral Procession
for Mr Lee Kuan Yew.

National Parks Board

**Address** Singapore Botanic Gardens Heritage Museum, entrance Tanglin Gate, 1 Cluny Road, Singapore 259569 (Tanglin) | **Getting there** Bus 7, 77, 106, 123, 174 from Orchard Boulevard to Opposite Botanic Gardens | **Hours** Daily 9am–6pm, closed every last Monday in the month; the affiliated CDL Green Gallery: daily 9am–6pm, closed every last Tuesday | **Tip** Left along Evans Road from the Nassim Gate exit you will find Mr. Prata, a paradise for Indian pancakes of all kinds.

# 4 Baba House

*The heritage of the Peranakan*

The way in is through a half-size, ornately carved swing door, the kind you see in the saloons of Western films. The actual door behind is usually open to let fresh air in. After all, the little swing door is enough to repel evil spirits – fortunately ghosts cannot get over barriers. Beyond the door is the antechamber, separated from the main room by a delicate wooden wall. Guests are received here, traditionally only members of the family enter the main room.

But we are allowed to proceed. This blue house in Tanjong Pagar on the edge of Chinatown is a jewel, open to the inquisitive. It is the only accessible house that reflects, with its construction and furnishings, the whole Peranakan way of life.

This ethnic group goes back to men from China who established families with Malay women. Babas are their male descendants; the females are Nonyas. Chinese, Malaysian and Western influences fused into an autonomous culture, which expresses itself in the architecture, art and in particular the cuisine of the Peranakan, which has grown in Singapore, but also in Malacca and Penang.

The blue house belonged to the Wee family, who grew rich as shipowners. It left this legacy, including the interior, to the National University of Singapore, in order that it be retained as a cultural monument. Today the house appears as it would have in the 1890s, as if its inhabitants had only just left it to go shopping. From the kitchen fittings to the living rooms and bedrooms – the world of the Peranakan comes to life here.

The woodwork on the house is from the Malaysian tradition, the animal ornaments made of ceramic fragments are Chinese, the painted tiles British. This style, grown out of three cultures, is what makes it so charming. Only the Peranakan cuisine, also known as Nonya cuisine, has made it into the modern world. Good food always survives after all, especially in Singapore.

**Address** 157 Neil Road, Singapore 088883 (Chinatown) | **Getting there** MRT to EW 16/NE 3 Outram Park | **Hours** Heritage Tours Tue – Fri 10am, book at babahouse.nus.edu.sg | **Tip** Blair Road, a small, quiet street, lined by wonderfully preserved shophouses, is a gem waiting to be discovered.

# 5 __ The Berlin Wall
*The wall is staying put!*

At the centre of this story: two concrete panels. The location: the garden behind the Tembusu College of the National University of Singapore. The date: 18 October, 2016. And there they stand, three men with serious expressions on their faces, thirty chosen guests and dozens of students. Right in the middle of it all: two panels of the Berlin Wall, sprayed with colourful graffiti. They are unveiled, and the principal of the college, the Singaporean Foreign Minister and the German ambassador make their speeches. The foreign office has loaned out these pieces of concrete, steeped in history, to the university for at least five years.

Will they feel at home here? As eyewitnesses of a distant city, of German history even, now here, deep in the tropics? They have already been away from home for a long time; in 1991 the German company Elmar Prost bought the two 3.6-metre-tall giants, each weighing four tonnes, as symbols of freedom and German reunification. Prost then presented them to the local foreign office on the occasion of the 50th anniversary of diplomatic relations between Germany and Singapore.

They have already experienced quite a lot. Fear, horror, desperation, death. They have been decorated, have seen tears of joy, they have been danced on in the frenzy of sudden freedom. They can tell the story of all this. And that is why they are here – the idea is that they should challenge Singaporean students to stop and think, to pose questions. Questions about a world with walls or a world with open borders. A world ruled by conflict and war or one with an open exchange of ideas and people.

There are pieces of the Berlin Wall in more than a hundred cities around the world. These two on the equator would seem to have landed on their feet. But ultimately it is time that will tell, as these two already know. And one day they will have even more to say.

Address In the garden behind the Tembusu College in University Town, 26 College Avenue East, Singapore 138597 (Clementi) | Getting there MRT to EW 21/CC 22 Buona Vista, then bus 196 to University Town, then on foot | Hours Always accessible | Tip The Lee Kong Chian Natural Museum at 2 Conservatory Drive looks like a massive lump of rock. The Raffles collection and a dinosaur family are hidden inside.

# 6___ The Billiard Table

*Wildlife in the jungle city*

In 1920, a tiger – escaped from a circus or straight out of the jungle – is supposed to have snuck its way into the highly respectable Raffles Hotel. There it lurked under the billiard table. The frightened waiter called the manager, a sharpshooter. But even he needed five bullets to slay the beast.

Those who now think that the modern metropolis has nothing animal to offer other than a slain tiger, its world-famous zoo and the delicacy 'frog in porridge' are completely and utterly wrong. Singapore is green. And where there's green, there's life.

The most hated are the mosquitoes, as some of them transmit the dreaded dengue fever. In order to drive them away, every part of the city is fogged out with insecticides once a week. But the tropical island awaits with a whole other calibre of threats and treats: packs of wild boar are forced into the suburbs time and again by hunger. Monkeys have pursued pupils of the German European School, among others, when they were lying in the middle of a thicket. The pupils have been given strict orders not to feed the funny but vicious creatures, as well as whistles to scare them away. A python managed to make its way into the toilet of a car-parts shop. Large lizards wait in the Botanic Gardens for the first rays of sun early in the morning. And in the nature parks a crocodile will appear now and then – even though Barney, the 400-kilogram saltwater crocodile from the Kranji Reservoir, passed away in mysterious circumstances in 2014. Singaporeans' favourites are still the cute otters, who enjoy the newly created wetlands.

But Singapore is, all things considered, a safe patch of earth in terms of its wildlife. In fact, a British woman was one of the last victims of a wild animal attack: a member of the Swiss Club (see ch. 96), she swam in its pool in the open sea off Katong in 1925 – and crossed paths with a shark.

Address Raffles Hotel, 1 Beach Road, Singapore 189673 (Colonial District) | Getting there MRT to NS25/EW13 City Hall | Hours The hotel and the hotel arcades will reopen in the second half of 2018. | Tip The Tiong Bahru Market is a typical wet market: everything is wet on the ground, everything is fresh. Fish, meat, fruit and vegetables downstairs, hawkers serving food upstairs.

# 7 _ Black-and-White Houses
*Fine living for colonial masters*

The ultimate in tropical living – whether in the middle of the city on Scott's Road, on Goodwood Hill, in Tanglin or on Nassim Road – the black-and-white houses with their black-and-white blinds are emblems of the colonial dream. They are supplemented by the rarer red-and-whites, which show bare bricks.

However, the houses do not seem in period in the urban environment, surrounded by modern high-rises. They only feel true to their original style in an English-style park landscape, as in Alexandra Park. Here the view opens out suddenly onto a delightful valley with lush green meadows and a sprinkling of properties.

The British colonial administration built these houses for their senior military personnel and the military doctors of the nearby Alexandra Hospital between 1905 and 1940. The style of the buildings brings together British, Malaysian and Chinese elements. The graphical black-and-white colour scheme and timber framing in Tudor style, sometimes more, sometimes less pronounced, are British colonial favourites, as are the Doric and Corinthian columns. The form of the roof with its ventilation system and the woodwork in order to ensure cooling in the oppressive heat are Malaysian. The houses also stand on columns, so that they don't sink in the mud during the monsoon season. The division of the rooms, from public area to private, is recreated from Chinese houses.

The black-and-whites, as they are lovingly called, were built at the lowest possible cost with local building materials: bricks fired in Singapore, floors and windows made of tropical wood, tiles and floor panels from China.

There is lots of light but little direct sunlight in the generously laid-out rooms, plastered in white with high ceilings. When all the windows and doors are open and your gaze sweeps over the green valley, it might feel as though Scarlett O'Hara had reached the tropics.

**Address** Alexandra Park, circuit passing Hyderabad Road, Canterbury Road, Winchester Road, Royal Road, Singapore 119578 (Telok Blangah) | **Getting there** MRT to CC 27 Labrador Park, then bus 963 to Hort Park | **Hours** Always accessible | **Tip** For art lovers: the Gillman Barracks gallery quarter offers lots of art, gallery nights and restaurants.

# 8  The Black Elephant

*The king's love of Singapore*

Why oh why is there a cute little bronze elephant on a pedestal in front of Old Parliament House? Tigers once roamed the island, and they call the metropolis 'The Lion City', but history lists no elephants here for commemoration.

By stepping a little closer, the interested observer can read the answer on the pedestal, written in four languages: Thai, Malay, Chinese and English. The elephant memorial is a gift from the former king of Siam to Singapore. With it he wanted to give thanks for his first visit in 1871.

King Somdetch Phra Paramindr Maha Chulalongkorn, or King Rama V for short, was a travel-loving and outgoing regent. Never before him did a Thai king venture outside his home country. Not even his father, who was played by Yul Brynner in the Hollywood film version of *The King and I*, and is very well known in the Western world.

His son loved Singapore. He visited often and brought many new, progressive ideas back with him to Thailand. The telephone, electricity, the railway, hospitals and last but not least the English language. The king, clearly modern for his time, brought the country into the 'Golden Age of Siam'. He even sent his children to study at the Raffles Institution, was a charitable donor and demonstrated great vision when he bought a piece of land on Orchard Road. His countrymen warned him against it and shook their heads behind his back. Today they could get down on their knees to thank him: located back then far out on the nutmeg plantations, the land is now in the middle of the city centre and is worth a fortune. It houses the Royal Thai Embassy.

The friendly little elephant should remind us of the king's love of Singapore. From his pedestal he looks out onto the Padang, the large square that was at the centre of the colonial city. He couldn't have chosen a more prominent place.

**Address** In front of Old Parliament House, 1 Old Parliament Lane, Singapore 179429 (Colonial District) | **Getting there** MRT to NS 25/EW 13 City Hall | **Tip** Local bands play at Timbre@The Arts House, behind Old Parliament House, while guests sit in the restaurant or the bar with a beautiful view of the Singapore River.

# 9 Bukit Brown Cemetery

*Almost lost to the jungle*

It is particularly nice to walk through this old Chinese cemetery in the light of the morning sun. Tall, shady jungle trees all over, the sounds of birds, otherwise peaceful tranquility, the sound of the traffic far off. An enchanted place.

There are paths, but most of the graves are hidden in the long grass to the left or right of them, often overgrown by the jungle, some well-kept, many ruinous. They are loosely spread out over the 200-hectare site without any apparent order, but are in fact positioned according to the rules of feng shui. There is a lot to discover here – wonderfully sculpted gravestones and lion figures, big names from Singapore's history, family traditions. There must have been over 100,000 graves since its beginning at the end of the 19th century, but tens of thousands have already been lost – this tradition-rich place is in danger of disappearing.

Land is very precious in Singapore, as it is strictly limited by its island status. The cemetery's huge area is to be used, bit by bit, for infrastructure projects. A new road is currently being laid out through the park, an MRT station constructed, and at some point tower blocks will rise up towards the sky here.

But the discussion as to what extent tradition must give way to modernity has also erupted in Singapore. The central cemeteries here have been slowly broken up for some time already. The Takashimaya shopping centre in the middle of Orchard Road, the neighbourhood of Tiong Bahru and the apartments on Mount Sophia are all built on former graves. The traditional burial will have to give way to cremation due to a lack of space.

However, many make the case for Bukit Brown being preserved as cultural heritage and converted into a park. An independent initiative offers tours through the cemetery, in order to preserve the stories of the graves and with them a piece of Singapore's history too.

Address 36C Lorong Halwa, Singapore 288305 (Bukit Timah) | **Getting there** MRT to CC 20 Farrer Road, then five stops with bus 93, 165, 852, 855 before Singapore Island Country Club, then walk over the pedestrian bridge towards Sime Road and Lorong Halwa | **Hours** Always open | **Tip** In MacRitchie Reservoir at the other end of the cemetery there are restaurants, circular walking trails and a kayak rental station.

# 10__Businesswoman's Mosque
*The leaning tower of Singapore*

This mosque, the Masjid Hajjah Fatimah, is something very special: it is one of the very few around the world to be named after a woman. Hajjah Fatimah was the Malay wife of a prince from Celebes, what is today Sulawesi in Indonesia. He came from the Bugis ethnic group of seafaring traders. The Bugis made Singapore into a flourishing trading city in the 19th century. The district of the city on the Rochor River where they lived is still named after them today.

After the early death of her husband, Hajjah Fatimah took over his commercial business – a rare and courageous step for a woman in that period. She was extremely successful and became very wealthy. But her house was burgled twice, and on the second time was burned to the ground. In thanks that she was unharmed during these catastrophes, Hajjah Fatimah had this mosque built, in 1845–46, where her house once stood.

Your attention will at first be drawn to the minaret. Is your vision crooked or is it the tower? Yes, it is the tower. Over the years it has tilted more and more to the side, and is now about six degrees off centre. Quite predictably, people lovingly call it the 'leaning tower of Singapore'.

The whole house of worship is a mix of styles, an East-West fusion as a testimony to Singapore's multicultural society. The minaret looks like a reproduction of the first clock tower of St Andrews Church in the Colonial District and has European influences with its Doric columns. The dome over the prayer room points to the Islamic influence, the glazed porcelain tiles on the windows and the woodwork are Chinese elements.

There can be no doubt: only a cosmopolitan, culturally engaged woman would build such a structure. At the same time, Hajjah Fatimah has never really left her residence: she was buried in the mausoleum of her mosque, side by side with her only daughter and her son-in-law.

**Address** 4001 Beach Road, Singapore 199584 (Kampong Glam) | **Getting there** MRT to CC5 Nicoll Highway | **Hours** Daily 9am–9pm | **Tip** There are extraordinary vintage souvenirs for sale at the Heritage Shop at 93 Jalan Sultan.

# 11 The Cathay Building
*Lost facade, lost life*

Seen prosaically it is a concrete art deco facade, completed in 1939, with 'Cathay' in illuminated letters attached to it vertically. But who wants to see the world so unromantically? Even though one of Singapore's many shopping centres is to be found behind this facade, the Cathay is actually a peep-box into the past. At one point this was Singapore's tallest building at 79.5 metres and housed the city's first air-conditioned cinema. Pilots even used it as an orientation point when flying in to the airport in Kalang. And a whole generation arranged to meet each other in the Cathay.

The Cathay in the 1930s must have been the equivalent of what is springing up out of the ground today as integrated resorts. At the time its owner, the Malaysian-born Loke Wan Tho, described it as a 'one-stop shop': people were expected to visit to shop, to go to the hairdressers, to eat, to watch a film and to visit the cabaret in the evening.

But the gloss soon rubbed off. The Japanese used the cinema during the occupation from 1942, to show their propaganda films twice a day. After the war the British admiral Louis Mountbatten relocated his headquarters here. Then the Cathay became a symbol of the mistakes in Singapore's development. The city approved the demolition of the historical building and had a 17-storey office building constructed on the vacant space. Only the art deco front was preserved – but now it looks terribly lost.

A small gallery on the second floor commemorates the story of the Loke family. They built a film empire around the Cathay, financed the first Malay colour film in Singapore, brought many stars to the city and promoted the Chinese film industry. But they too did not have long to enjoy the building: Loke, his wife Mavis and several of his managers were killed in a plane crash in 1964. They were on their way to the Asian film festival in Taiwan.

Address 2 Handy Road, Singapore 229233 (Bugis) | Getting there MRT to NS 24/ NE 6/CC 1 Dhoby Ghaut | Hours Cathay Gallery: Level 2, Mon–Sat 11am–7pm | Tip The imposing SOTA (School Of The Arts) building on the right was built by WOHA, one of Singapore's renowned architectural offices, incorporating all the new trends: natural building materials and ventilation as well as vertical vegetation.

# 12 — The Changi Mural Copies
*The forgotten painter*

Before the war, Stanley Warren had painted giant film posters for the British Grenada Cinemas. His art also interested the army. In 1940 they engaged him to create sketches of possible targets. This is how the young painter ended up in the colony of Singapore two years later.

Here he was imprisoned with members of the Allied army. He was bound into forced labour, building roads, by the Japanese occupiers, but he managed to continue painting too, working in mixed media on the asbestos panels in Bukit Batok prison camp chapel. When he was transferred into the military hospital of the huge Changi camp, he demanded paints and a Bible, in order that he could resume his mural painting there.

Many guests to Singapore know 'Changi', for one as the name of the world-class airport. Others dread it, because this is where the prison is to be found, while those who are interested in the history of the Pacific region cannot help but think of the prisoner of war camp. More than 50,000 Australians, Brits and other Allied soldiers suffered here during the war in terribly inhumane conditions.

Warren's fellow prisoners provided him – sometimes at the risk of death – with wall paint, camouflage paint, crushed billiard chalk, and in this way he created five, three-metre-tall scenes including the birth of Christ, in St Luke's Chapel in Block 151. When the Japanese turned the blocks into sheds for the enlarged airport, the pictures were painted over and faded into oblivion.

Warren returned home after the war and became a teacher. The sheds became dorm rooms of the Royal Air Force. It wasn't until 1959 that the pictures were rediscovered. After a successful search for the painter, Stanley returned to Singapore three times to restore them. The originals still remain on the air base and are not open to the public, but replicas can be found in the Changi Chapel & Museum memorial site.

Address Changi Chapel & Museum, 1000 Upper Changi Road North, Singapore 507707 (Changi), www.changimuseum.sg | Getting there MRT to EW 4 Tanah Merah, then bus 2 to Changi Women's Prison | Hours Daily 9.30am–5pm, tours can be booked online | Tip The Coastal Settlement (200 Netheravon Road, www.thecoastalsettlement.com) is furnished like a retro museum, and the food is a mix of savoury Western and local flavours.

# 13 Chan Hou Meng's Takeaway

*A soya chicken reaches for the stars*

The name may sound complicated to non-Chinese ears: 'Liao Fan Hong Kong Soya Sauce Chicken Rice & Noodle'. But you had better get used to it. If things go according to the plans of its founder, Chan Hou Meng, his takeaway stall in the Chinatown Complex Market & Food Centre will become an international brand, like McDonald's or Kentucky Fried Chicken, within a few years.

Chan certainly has what it takes. This has now been officially confirmed. The chef became the first hawker in Singapore to be awarded with a Michelin star in July 2016 for his soya chicken. The 51-year-old almost bursts at the seams with pride – a few months after the commendation, he reports, five investors had already made contact with him, in the hope of persuading him to sell his recipe and his stall. But the negotiators of international hotels and food companies didn't know Chan very well – he knows what he and his soya chicken are worth. He wants 'at least two million Singapore dollars' – over one million pounds sterling – for his recipe. And on top of that, he wants a guarantee that the quality of his chicken will not suffer when it goes around the world in mass production.

High demands. But not for a star chef. At least the turnover at his little stall has tripled to more than 160 chickens a day due to the award, Chan says. Today, guests have to wait in line for up to two hours to try it.

Chan picked up the recipe in Hong Kong, when he worked there as a cook in 1989. But of course he has refined it with secret ingredients. 'It was always my dream to position my business internationally and to pass it on to the next generation,' says the starred-chef behind the takeaway counter. He has almost realised it. Today, 90 per cent of his customers are tourists. 'And they like it,' says Chan. 'So my soya chicken will also be received well all around the world.'

Address 335 Smith Street, Suite 02-126, Chinatown Complex Market & Food Centre, Singapore 050335 (Chinatown) | Getting there MRT to NE 4/DT 19 Chinatown | Hours Daily 10am–5pm | Tip A place for the renewed love for long-play records that Singapore is experiencing too: Hear Records at 5 Banda Street offers well-organised treasures.

# 14 Chesed-El Synagogue
*A home away from home*

Quite naturally, Jews also wanted to have their own house of worship in this foreign land. They established Singapore's first synagogue in a small office building in 1841. It was located in today's Synagogue Street and served the growing community for 37 years. In 1878, the Maghain Aboth in Waterloo Street was built, with its prayer hall oriented towards Jerusalem. It is considered one of the oldest Jewish buildings in Southeast Asia.

Singapore was a node of the Jewish diaspora from very early on. Jewish traders came to India, Burma and the Straits Settlements all along the road from Malacca with the British East India Company, which tapped the region for its trade and power aspirations. The community grew rapidly from only nine members in 1830 to at least a thousand members at the start of the last century. They even published their own newspapers, *Israelight* and the *Jewish Herald*.

In this heyday of the Jewish community, Manasseh Meyer, who had become rich through trading opium and real estate, built the Chesed-El Synagogue on the estate of his private residence on Oxley Rise.

His house, according to his guest Albert Einstein, was like a 'palace', the host like a 'Croesus'. Meyer's daughter Moselle Nissim, however, greatly impressed the Nobel-prizewinner-to-be: her's was 'one of the most beautiful faces of a Jewish woman' that he had ever seen. Moselle Meyer later made a name for herself as a benefactress from Singapore to Palestine.

Singapore's first chief administrator, David Marshall, also helped his fellow believers: in 1956 he convinced the then Chinese prime minister Zhou Enlai to allow more than 500 Jews of Russian descent to leave the country. Other famous Jews of Singapore include the businessmen F. J. Benjamin and Victor Sassoon: the first brought Gucci to Singapore; the second, The Coffee Bean & Tea Leaf.

חסד-אל

Address 2 Oxley Rise, Singapore 238693 (Colonial District), +65 8641 3570, www.chesedel.org | Getting there MRT to NS 24/NE 6/CC 1 Dhoby Ghaut | Hours By prior arrangement | Tip The beautiful Fort Canning Park is an extremely historical hill for Singapore: here are the archaeological excavations of past Malay kings.

# 15 The Children Sculptures
*The literary quartet*

The four of them sit and lie there in the shade, reading. But in fact you can hardly see them, because they are below street level. The huge new build of the national library in the Colonial District has granted them a tiny bamboo garden there. It is in the basement, behind a glass wall off the room for book returns. No sign, no poster points out the garden. You will only see it from the road if you bend over the railings on Middle Road and look into the depths.

But it's worth making the effort! Singaporean sculptor Chong Fah Cheong has installed four bronze children absorbed in their books, entitled *Once Upon a Time*, down there. They sit, they lie, they sprawl in life size, and seem so real on their white marble blocks, as though you had just pushed open the door to the nursery.

Making this kind of realistic artwork is Chong Fah Cheong's strength. The artist, who is a self-taught sculptor, has been allowed to place his work on many other corners of the city. The most famous of his sculptures is the five boys jumping into the Singapore River at the side of the Fullerton Hotel. Also bronze, that sculpture is called *First Generation*. Chong Fah Cheong now lives in Canada, but is adored in Singapore and is highly decorated. But very few people know his reading children.

The quartet of readers is at least as expressive as the wall in front of which the four browse. It is built of 5,000 red bricks, with a bamboo framework in front of it, recovered from the old National Library on Stamford Road. Opened in 1960, that library was a symbol for the development of their city for Singaporeans. Many have still not forgiven the state for tearing it down in the year 2000 in order to create space for the campus of the Singapore Management University. These bricks are all that remain from the old National Library. In front of them, the four children create their own world, immersed in their books.

**Address** National Library, 100 Victoria Street, Singapore 188064 (Bugis) | **Getting there** MRT to EW 12/DT 14 Bugis | **Hours** Daily 10am–9pm | **Tip** The Kwan Im Thong Hood Cho Temple in Waterloo Street is a beautiful place for living Buddhism and always full of believers.

# 16_ The Chinese Cultural Centre

*Dream in three pieces*

Chinese cultural events were actually supposed to play the main role in this new build. But the main role is already assigned – to the building itself. Bold yet subtle, it connects Chinese tradition with modernity.

At first it seems more like a fortress, a closed monumental block. Those who venture closer will discover how open this building actually is. The concept of the building by Singapore's DP Architects follows the Chinese tradition of the division of the universe into heaven, earth and man. The earth is symbolised by the two-storey base. From the street you enter it unhindered through a columned space that is open on three sides. You are instinctively reminded of a temple entrance.

Monumental stairways and hidden rooms open out in the floor above. Time and again the architects refer back to classic Chinese tones – in particular with the sealing-wax red cubes in the central block and the subdued gold. But here they are not used in the traditional, opulently ornamental way – they are sparingly deployed, sometimes two-dimensional, sometimes textural. Like an ink drawing with coloured accents.

Further up in the red central block, all of the event rooms are housed over four storeys. This part symbolises man. Plain but elegant materials, modern interpretations of Chinese wooden structures and time and again this astonishing spaciousness – an aesthetic dream is summoned. And then, even higher, comes the roof of the building representing heaven: a garden laid out according to classic Chinese dimensions with leafy red trees and surprising visual axes. Not visible from the outside, it offers a staggering panorama view of the coastal land.

The building's complexity is only completely revealed at night however: the monumental building is almost transparent, and the red mass in the central block glows like a heart in a glass body.

**Address** 1 Straits Boulevard, Singapore 018906 (Central Business District) | **Getting there** MRT to DT 17 Downtown | **Hours** Mon–Fri 9am–6pm, except during events | **Tip** Ladies Night is every Wednesday from 6 to 10pm in the Exchange Bar in Asia Square (8–12 Marina View) with free margaritas and a clear view of the many businessmen…

# 17_The Chinese Store

*Lift to China*

The merchandise is still well organised here. Background musak? Nope. Tables full of special offers? Not necessary. Branded clothes? None in sight. Instead: real silk cheongsams, the traditional Chinese festive dress; silk jackets and trousers; silk nightclothes and underwear too. With the friendly help of well-trained ladies of an older vintage, the type that seems to have disappeared since the golden age of the department store back home, there are still treasures to be found at Yue Hwa.

The whole store gives the impression that socialism is still running its merry little course. To the right of the entrance is traditional Chinese medicine. Here you will find teas and ingredients that no one in the West even knows. The apothecaries put the remedies together according to your prescription.

In the past things were much more luxurious on what are now rather sober floors – today's Yue Hwa Chinese Products Emporium was once the Chinese Great Southern Hotel, the Raffles of China-town. Opened by the wealthy businessman Lum Chang in 1936, it was the first Chinese luxury hotel with a lift in Singapore. Renowned cabarets, dance bars and the Chinese Opera entertained the paying guests. This was where the Chinese rich and beautiful and film stars from Hong Kong would let their hair down at lively parties and in the trendiest Chinese shops.

The hotel's decline began with the upheaval in China and the changing taste in music towards rock 'n' roll – the illustrious guests were replaced by normal tourists from Malaysia and Indonesia, the famous cabaret and the dance bars closed. The Hong Kong department store chain Yue Hwa eventually bought the ramshackle building in 1993, restored its heritage-protected facade, but completely changed the interior design. But the building still seems to have that certain atmosphere, that hint of a long lost time.

Address 70 Eu Tong Sen Street, Singapore 059805 (Chinatown) | Getting there MRT to NE 4/DT 19 Chinatown | Hours Sun–Fri 11am–9pm, Sat 11am–10pm | Tip The Spring Court at 52–56 Upper Cross Street is the oldest family-run restaurant in Singapore. Chinese dishes have been cooked here to family recipes since 1929.

# 18__ The Civilian War Memorial

*Four towers for eternity*

It is known as the 'Chopstick Memorial'. But harmless as the name sounds, the four concrete pillars that tower 68 metres high and are indeed reminiscent of Chinese chopsticks at first sight, form a war memorial of a different kind. With it, Singapore commemorates the civilian victims of the Japanese occupation during World War II. The comparison with chopsticks isn't at all indecent in Singapore: the two towers of the Takashimaya shopping complex have likewise been compared with them, as have the three towers of the new casino complex, Marina Bay Sands.

The pillars of the memorial stand for four ethnicities: Chinese, Malaysian, Indian and other ethnicities, who suffered under the Japanese occupation between 1942 and 1945. The atrocities went as low as displaying the heads of shot civilians in public. It has been estimated that the occupiers killed around 50,000 civilians. In mid-February 1962, five mass graves were discovered in Siglap, later a further 40 were uncovered. For many years Singapore's Chinese Chamber of Commerce was responsible for maintaining the memory of the victims and for following their stories. After the war, the ashes of those whose remains were picked up in the Changi Prison and in places of execution such as Siglap were laid to rest in a burial chamber under the memorial.

The government provided the space for the park in the heart of Singapore and also assumed half of the building costs. The other half was contributed by the Chamber of Commerce. During the inauguration of the memorial in 1963, the now legendary Lee Kuan Yew, prime minister at the time, said: 'As painful as the past was, we must live and plan for the future, without being hindered by it. We cannot forget, cannot completely forgive, but we can soothe the wounds that eat away at so many hearts.'

**Address** War Memorial Park, Beach Road, opposite Raffles City, Singapore 068912
(Colonial District) | **Getting there** MRT to CC2 Esplanade | **Hours** Always accessible |
**Tip** Indulge yourself: the Golden Peony restaurant in Conrad Centennial Hotel one
street on offers superior Chinese cuisine.

# 19— The Club of Songbirds

*The tropical bird singing contest*

One of the most popular pets of the 1960s, the budgerigar, with its mirror and spray of millet, has all but disappeared from our living rooms. But at the Kebun Baru Bird Singing Club, they and many other varieties of songbird are all the rage. Hundreds of elaborately carved birdcages hang up high on poles in a large field between HDB blocks, so that the precious songbirds inside get plenty of air and light.

And what a range of feathered friends there is! There's the shama, which can be very expensive indeed, its value depending on the quality of its song or the frequency of its feather movements while singing. The jambul with its black hood and red patch and white circle under its eyes. The mata puteh, small and very cute, also with a white ring under its eyes. All of them sing beautifully, but the most beautiful song of all is the merbok's. It can be recognised by the blue of its beak, head and cheeks and the black-and-white-striped ruff. They can cost up to 100,000 Singapore dollars.

The birds are brought here by their owners to train their singing from around six in the morning. The greater the number of birds, the more animated they become. The club is at its busiest at the weekend between 10 and 11am, before it gets too hot around noon. There are also big singing competitions, during which over 1,000 poles are occupied. The air is filled with warbling, chirping and tweeting as the judges go from pole to pole, equipped with pen and clipboard, to assess the timbre, length and endurance of the singing.

On the days without competition, a meditative tranquility that belongs to the birds and their song alone envelops the field. Even if you find the cages disturbing and would prefer to see birds in their natural habitat, you can't help but be moved by the symphony of their soft sounds in the wind. And by the dedication of the owners to their pets.

Address Ang Mo Kio Avenue 5, Block 159, Singapore 560159 (Ang Mo Kio) | **Getting there** MRT to NS 16 Ang Mo Kio, then bus 138, 269 to Block 151. Follow the path between Blocks 151 and 152, along the open field of the Ang Mo Kio West Park to the club opposite Block 159. | **Hours** Daily 6am–5pm, at best on Sundays | **Tip** The beautiful Bishan-Ang Mo Kio Park (1384 Ang Mo Kio Avenue 1) was created from a re-natured canal – an eco-project undertaken by the company Dreiseitl from Lake Constance.

# 20 The Coffee Alphabet

*First spell, then enjoy*

Those who just want to drink coffee go to Starbucks. But that would be a real mistake in Singapore, where it is much more fun to familiarise yourself with the local coffee alphabet and watch the coffee makers behind the bar at work.

One café is called Killiney Kopitiam. If you simply ask for a coffee in English here, you may be fobbed off with a cup of Nescafé. If you order a *kopi*, you'll be handed a 'real' coffee, often lightened with condensed milk. However, those who are used to slurping their caffeine in modern coffee chains will find it served here in rather homeopathic doses: in a small cup, only a little bigger than a mocha cup. The *kopi* is at its most original when it has been brewed using robusta beans roasted in butter or margarine, and is served in thick porcelain cups. The original ones are white with a green floral pattern and still can be found in some *kopitiams*.

But in order to get a *kopi* the way you want it, you really have to learn to juggle with the alphabet: plain and black is *kopi O*. *Kopi C* is sweetened coffee with condensed milk, whereas if you ask for *kopi C kosong* it comes with condensed milk, but unsweetened. *Kopi C siew tai* has less sugar. *Kopi peng* is coffee cooled down for the tropical climate with ice. The crowning glory is *kopi C peng*. Yes, you guessed it: iced, with condensed milk and sugar – the height of emotion for coffee lovers on the equator.

If all of the different names have made you dizzy, just wait until you see how the stuff is made. The roasted coffee is first brewed for a long time with boiling water in a coffee net inside a tin can. In order to add as much air as possible, the barista pours the hot coffee from one can into a second in a high arch and then back into the net in an equally high arch. After repeating this several times the coffee is now dark brown. Finally it is poured with great gusto into the cups and finished off with more hot water.

**Address** Killiney Kopitiam, 67 Killiney Road, Singapore 239525 (Centre) | Getting there MRT to NS 23 Somerset | Hours Mon, Wed–Sat 6am–11pm, Tue & Sun 6am–6pm | Tip On Robertson Quay 41 is the renowned STPI, formerly Singapore Tyler Print Institute, which offers workshops and art exhibitions on the theme of printing and paper (www.stpi.com.sg).

# 21　Corner House

*Simian treetop scavengers*

Monkeys defined his life, or at least, played a hugely important role in it: a British botanist in the service of Singapore, Edred John Henry Corner used the primates to his benefit, and they may have saved his life too.

But let's take one thing at a time. Corner went down in Singaporean history because he ran the old Botanic Gardens from 1929 to 1945. The highly decorated scientist was ingenious. In 1937, he managed to find a way to reach the tops of tropical trees and helped to establish research in this hard-to-reach area. To this end, Corner made use of agile comrades – he bought trained macaque monkeys. Villagers at that time trained them to pick coconuts. The scientist taught them to bring down seeds, fruit, ferns and leaves from 50-metre-high trees. Corner was so successful in this that he even secured money for his project from the British colonial administration: each monkey was funded with 127 Singapore dollars of taxes a year.

The relationship between man and monkey must have been good. The climbing artistes were given Malay names and were kept in good spirits with rice, bananas and raw eggs. However, old photos testify that they were forced to wear long chains, so that they wouldn't make off with their treetop haul. This carried on until 1942, when the Japanese invaded Singapore, and Corner set his monkeys free. Perhaps they thanked him in their own very unique way: one of the monkeys bit the researcher in the right arm, which was then largely paralysed. What at first sounds like dreadful misfortune may well have saved Corner's life: the crippled arm saved him from being locked up in the infamous Changi Prison, where many Allies lost their lives.

Today the Corner House in the Botanic Gardens named after him commemorates the great researcher. The black-and-white house built in 1910 houses a first-class restaurant of the same name.

**Address** Botanic Gardens, 1 Cluny Road, Singapore 259569 (Tanglin), +65 64691000 |
**Getting there** MRT to CC 19/DT 9 Botanic Gardens, or by taxi to Nassim Gate | **Hours**
Tue – Sat noon – 3pm & 6.30 – 11pm, Sun 11.30am – 3pm & 6.30 – 11pm | **Tip** Cluny
Court is opposite MRT Botanic Gardens. Here you can enjoy cold drinks and Italian
coffee and stroll through Singaporean, French and Swedish boutiques.

# 22— The David Elias Building

*Love under the Star of David*

The Star of David shines down from the gable ends and the two side walls: the David Elias Building from 1928 displays clearly that its builder was of the Jewish faith. The eponymous businessman commissioned its building by the colonial architects Swan & Maclaren, who had also built the Teutonia Club, today the Goodwood Park Hotel, and the Sultan Mosque. The Sun Sun Hotel was temporarily housed in the office building.

The Jews in emergent Singapore were divided into two classes. The rich lived on the edge of the city like the colonial rulers. Most of the Sephardic Jews from Baghdad, on the other hand, stayed in the quarter around the Elias and the nearby Ellison Building, which also has a Star of David on its gable. In the 'Mahallah' (Arabic for 'neighbourhood') there was kosher food as well as all the local gossip. As well as the stately yellow office building, the Elias family owned land and a bungalow in Pasir Ris. Amber Road is named after Amber Elias; Elias Road, which once led to their holiday home, is named after their sons, Joseph and Ezra.

The Elias family arranged a wedding for their 18-year-old daughter, Rebecca, with a Sephardic Jew – a man who was admittedly much older than her. As is the way in such situations, Rebecca lost her heart to another. David Frankel was good looking, possessing everything a heartbreaker needs, but belonged to Singapore's Ashkenazi Jewish community. It therefore took a long time and cost many tears until mama Elias finally agreed to the love match. The affluence of the Frankels, in no way inferior to that of the Elias family, may well have helped. In the faded black-and-white photographs of Albert Einstein's visit in 1922, the Frankels are standing right next to Manasseh Meyer, the uncrowned king of the Jewish community (see ch. 14). They had earned their money with a furniture store and also owned large coconut plantations.

Address 270 Middle Road, Singapore 188993 (Bugis) | Getting there MRT to EW 12/ DT 14 Bugis | Hours Can only be viewed from the outside | Tip The architecture of the nearby Lasalle College of the Arts is interesting, and its lively student café, Lower Case, is open to everyone.

# 23__ The Duo High Rises
*Arabian nights*

This man casts fairy tales in concrete. And Singapore likes them. That's why the German star architect Ole Scheeren has already built two huge residential and office buildings in Singapore. Many of his colleagues have also left their mark on the city: the late Zaha Hadid, Daniel Libeskind, Christoph Ingenhoven and of course Sir Norman Foster.

Singapore realised around the turn of the century that it needed more than low tax rates and good hospitals to rise up to the status of world metropolis. Built statements were needed. Buildings that cause the beholder to gaze up into the sky, whose photographs would circle the world.

One has been particularly good at that: Mosche Safdie's Marina Bay Sands, whose rooftop pool is considered the most photographed in the world. But the city has many more architectural icons to offer. Foster crowned the Supreme Court with one of his domes, like the Reichstag building in Berlin before it. Then South Beach followed, in the heart of the city opposite Raffles Hotel, where Hadid placed three towers (at first hard to sell because Singaporeans found them too expensive) in one of the best residential areas of the city. And Libeskind created a poetic ensemble with Reflections on Keppel Bay, which seems to sway like grass in the sea breeze.

But Scheeren is the best storyteller. The man from Karlsruhe built up a tower of what look like enormous bricks near the harbour – the residential complex The Interlace looks like the result of a giant baby playing with Lego. It was World Building of the Year in 2015. While this was built in collaboration with the office of his former employee Rem Kohlhaas, Duo, a pair of towers on the edge of the Arab quarter, is his own work. Their *Arabian Nights* sort of glow is no surprise: Duo was financed by Singapore's sovereign wealth fund Temasek and the Malaysian sovereign wealth fund Khazanah.

Address Fraser Street, Singapore 189352 (Bugis) | Getting there MRT to EW12/
DT14 Bugis | Hours 10am–9pm | Tip Souvenirs of a very different kind: Supermama at
265 Beach Road offers many other hand-picked products by Japanese and Singaporean
artists alongside its porcelain Singapore icon series.

# 24__ The Durian Stall

*A smelly green monster with prickly skin*

Red metal stools. A striped awning. A stench.

Or is it a pleasure? That depends on your perspective. The smell we're talking about is that of the durian, also lovingly called 'stinky fruit'. Some love the taste of this emblematic fruit, but everyone finds it stinky.

The light-green beast with its crocodile-skin spikes can be bought on many corners of the city, but when it's in season, why not take a trip to Tanglin Village? This is actually an overpriced entertainment district for nighttime revellers, but all the way at the back to the right, past the Indian restaurant and then down a dead-end street, is a paradise for durian lovers. A little stall, prettified at night with a string of lights, offers varieties such as Gold Phoenix, Mao Shan Wang or Hong Xia, which means nothing other than 'red crab', but tastes very different.

Wan Li Xiang, now in his late eighties, founded his stall in the 1950s. Back then, he explains, there were several other durian sellers here on Dempsey Hill; today they are 'all dead'. Around three every afternoon he receives his delivery; by eight in the evening it is all sold out. Wan's big plus point: he is one of the few still selling durians from Pulau Ubin. The island is considered Singapore's green corner and is well known for its fruit the size of footballs.

Once you've chosen your fruit and paid Mr Wan, it's best to eat your durian right here on the tables in front of the stall. You aren't allowed to take the green monsters with you on the train or bus, nor into the theatre or cinema. You probably wouldn't even want the 'king of fruit' in your own car. The smell, which reminds some people of overripe Camembert, is too pungent. In order to be able to enjoy their national fruit nonetheless, Singaporeans bake it into biscuits, add it to milkshakes or serve it with sticky rice. Not to everyone's taste, but definitely less stinky!

**Address** 7 Dempsey Road, Singapore 249684 (Tanglin) | **Getting there** Bus 7, 75, 77, 105, 106, 123, 174 to After Peirce Road | **Hours** Daily 3pm–midnight | **Tip** London, New York, Tokyo, Beijing – and now Singapore too: the Dover Street Market, a few buildings away, presents 15 selected international fashion labels in a very unusual way.

# 25 — Einstein Memorial Plaque

*First supplicant, then Nobel prizewinner*

When Albert Einstein disembarked from the Japanese steamship *Kitano Maru* in Singapore harbour on the morning of Thursday the 2nd of November 1922 with his wife, Elsa, he was after money. Many Jews in Singapore – the census referred to 623 – were wealthy, and Einstein was petitioning the Jewish community in the colonial city to help finance a Hebraic university in Jerusalem.

A crowd of admirers awaited the 43-year-old celebrity from Germany. 'The great scientist and his wife were welcomed by the leading members of the Jewish community', reported *The Straits Times*. Einstein mentioned in his notes that he was 'greeted cordially by Zionists'.

The physician became acquainted with tropical affluence. He was impressed by Abraham Frankel's coconut plantation. The philanthropist had other land holdings as well, one of which he developed in the 1960s into the present Opera Estate residential neighbourhood, whose paths he christened Aida, Carmen and Fidelio. Einstein had no cause to feel foreign: his hosts were the Montors, the family of an ethnic German diamond merchant, who could talk with Einstein in his mother tongue. But the guest complained in secret that Alfred Montor's welcoming speech was rigid and overloaded with phrases.

Einstein suffered all courtesies in order not to endanger his purpose: his main target was the ultra-rich Manasseh Meyer (see ch. 14), an orthodox Jew, who lived from the trade in opium and real estate. His house, according to Einstein, was like a 'palace', the host like a 'Croesus'.

'I don't know whether any of my rockets pierced Croesus' thick skin,' Einstein wrote, concerned he'd been unsuccessful. But when the newly announced Nobel prizewinner stopped off in Singapore again in January 1923, the newspapers reported that Manasseh Meyer had contributed 500 pounds and the Jewish community 250 pounds for the university.

**Address** Upper East Coast Road, opposite the Jalan Tua Kong in front of the public car park, Singapore 455208 (Bedok) | **Getting there** MRT to CC 8 Dakota, then bus 10 to Opposite Springvale | **Hours** Always accessible | **Tip** East Coast Park along the seashore is great for walking, cycling, skating and good food.

# 26 Eng Aun Tong Factory

*The leaping tiger cures the pain*

Neck ache? Back pains? Pounding head? No problem. We're in Singapore, home of the viscous orange ointment that seems to work magic against all ailments: Tiger Balm. The balm is sold in more than a hundred countries in its iconic octagonal glass jar.

No, it's not originally from Singapore, but this is where it grew up. It was first mixed by a pharmacist at the imperial court in Peking. Around 1870 his son Aw Chu Kin moved to Rangoon in Burma, a vibrant British trading post at the time. There he founded a pharmacy – Eng Aun Tong ('Hall of Eternal Peace') – where he mixed pastes and tinctures. His sons refined the recipe to create Tiger Balm. Later, having already grown rich, they relocated the business to Singapore.

The factory was built in a neoclassical style in Chinatown in 1924 – today the Goethe Institute is housed directly opposite – and the Aws mixed their balm of methanol, camphor, cinnamon, peppermint and cloves, bottled it in octagonal jars sealed with a gold-coloured lid and the famous orange label with the leaping tiger here from then on. The factory building, which also housed eBay for a while at the start of this century, is particularly notable for its roof: it was one of the first buildings in Singapore with a flat roof. More importantly, it has a little tower on the street-facing side. Being octagonal, it resembles the balm's hexagonal jars. The name of the building too made sure that its purpose was clear to all: the words 'The Tiger Medical Hall' were affixed resplendently above the main doors.

Success came quickly. Soon the Aws built a factory that was ten times bigger in the Jurong industrial zone. Their company was sold on several times over the following decades. But over time Tiger Balm grew to be considered an old-fashioned ointment. Marketing experts ultimately helped the tiger back to its feet, making the balm into a lifestyle product.

Address 89 Neil Road, Singapore 088849 (Chinatown) | Getting there MRT to EW16/ NE 3 Outram Park | Hours Can only be viewed from outside | Tip You can take part in drop-in meditation on Tuesdays, Wednesdays and Fridays at the Kadampa Meditation Centre opposite (+65 64381127).

# 27__The ERP Gantry

*Pay when it beeps*

Singapore is a car-centric city. Or maybe not? You only have to go to the Conrad Hotel to see the orange or bright green sports cars, all parked up in a neat line. At the same time, driving in the tropical metropolis is more expensive than in most other cities on the planet.

Anyone who is anyone doesn't only have a Bentley, but a Ferrari for the weekend too. They take it for trips to neighbouring Malaysia where they can really open up – distances are short and the roads are full in the city state. But even at a snail's pace you can show that you can afford to spend a six-figure sum on a set of wheels.

But everyone who vegetates below the Ferrari-Lamborghini-Maserati salary bracket groans at the high costs. To start with there is the licence, then there are the steep parking fees and finally the money sucked up under one of these huge grey gantries that span every arterial road in the inner city. Every vehicle in Singapore must carry a debit card in a reader on the dashboard, which beeps every time the car passes through a gantry. A fee is deducted from it with every beep for entry into the city centre. The vehicle number is recorded by flash photography, and the price, which varies according to the volume of traffic and can be up to two Singapore dollars, flashes up on the gantry. So residents are encouraged to change to buses, trains, the taxis with their sometimes aged drivers or the nowadays omnipresent bicycles.

The large grey gantry at the upper end of Orchard Road is like a gateway into a shopping paradise. Only those who pay are let in. Singapore has used ERP, Electronic Road Pricing, since 1998. But the days of the gantries are numbered: soon the system will be switched to a satellite-based GPS, that not only calculates entry, but also records the length of your stay in the city centre to the minute. This will make things fairer, but certainly not cheaper.

Address Over Orchard Road at the junction of Scotts Road and Paterson Road (Centre) | Getting there MRT to NS 22 Orchard | Hours Always accessible | Tip In the basement of the shopping palace ION Orchard you will find Tori Q, a Japanese grill, where meat is grilled on skewers using a fascinating machine. Watch out: the sauce is addictive (#B 4-53).

# 28__The Former Ford Factory
*Two days under the wrong name*

Sometimes you want to keep everyone happy – but still manage to do the opposite. That's what happened with the Old Ford Factory. The first factory in Southeast Asia producing cars by the American manufacturer is as such already a piece of contemporary history. Its significance is a very different one for Singaporeans however. In February 1942, the then British colonial rulers capitulated inside these walls and handed over control to the Japanese victors. Three dreadful years of Japanese crimes against the Singaporean civilian population followed, which shape the collective memory of the city state to this day.

All of this is well known, and was reflected in an exhibition about World War II and the 'darkest hours in Singapore's modern history', displayed in the Ford Factory for many years. But then it was modified, with the intention of making it more modern and realistic. This went hand in hand with a change of name: 'Syonan Gallery – War and its Legacies'. But a storm of protest immediately followed, as 'Syonan-to', 'Light of the South Island', was the name the Japanese gave to Singapore during the period of occupation. The word brought back traumatic memories for Singaporeans. So the gallery was only called 'Syonan' for two days. On the Friday after the opening the government declared that due to the protests, particularly online, the exhibition would from now on operate under the name 'Surviving The Japanese Occupation – War and its Legacies'. Prime Minister Lee Hsien Loong said: 'Quite a few felt that the name itself, used like this, caused them pain. Many Singaporeans of all races suffered terrible atrocities during the Japanese Occupation, or had family members who did,' And so the Old Ford Factory, 75 years after closing, became not only a symbol of the abomination of the war, but also of the swift adaptability of the city-state's government.

ORD FACTORY

Address 351 Upper Bukit Timah Road, Singapore 588192 (Bukit Timah) | Getting there MRT to DT 3 Hillview, then bus 67, 170, 171, 961 to Opposite The Hillside | Hours Daily 9am–5.30pm, guided tours at www.nas.gov.sg/formerfordfactory | Tip The café-restaurant Spruce Firestation at number 260 in the same street is housed in the former fire engine hall.

# 29 The Gandhi Memorial

*The final journey of the father of India*

Anti-colonial tendencies were on the rise in Singapore after World War I. And so the Indian nationalists of the day, such as Pandit Jawaharlal Nehru, who would later be the prime minister of India, and Netaji Subhas Chandra Bose, who directed his resistance movement from Singapore, were able to bring together crowds of people here, as did the Indian winner of the Nobel Prize in Literature, Rabindranath Tagore. It's no surprise that the large Indian diaspora also revered Gandhi.

Gandhi never actually made it to the island during his lifetime. However, a portion of his ashes were flown to Singapore after the cremation of his body, so that they could be brought out to the Indian communities of the region. After the urn's return from Ipoh in today's Malaysia, it was carried in a procession through the city on 27 March, 1948. Because the sea was too rough to sail out far, the urn was taken aboard a small boat at Clifford Pier, with a canopy that was decorated with flowers. Five girls sang Gandhi his favourite song 'Raghupathi Raghava Raja Ram' one more time. The delegate from the Indian government then mixed the ashes with water from the Ganges, before he consigned them to the sea. The people on over 20 boats that had sailed out to the mouth of the Singapore River tried as quickly as they could to fill bowls with seawater from around the boat, to secure themselves a souvenir. An airplane circled above the scene for more than an hour, scattering rose petals. Meanwhile thousands bowed on the shore, paying their last respects to their idol.

Two years later Nehru laid the foundation stone for the Mahatma Gandhi Memorial Hall on the edge of Little India. The population had donated a good 100,000 Singapore dollars for its construction. A bust in the hall and a relief on its outer wall keep the memory of the subcontinent's father alive.

**Address** 3 Race Course Lane, Singapore 218731 (Little India) | **Getting there** MRT to NE 8 Farrer Park | **Hours** Always accessible | **Tip** Sweet and fatty: in the Moghul Sweet Shop in the Little India Arcade (48 Seragoon Road) you will find all of those wickedly delicious Indian sweets that you simply have to try.

# 30__The Gate of Hope
*Singapore's baby hatch*

The door on the corner of the former French convent at the junction of Bras Basah Road and Victoria Street appears inconspicuous. But for a long time this door pledged the chance of life.

The Catholic father Jean-Marie Beurel founded the girl's school Convent of the Holy Infant Jesus (CHIJ), which was run by French nuns, in 1854. A part of the school was an orphanage, where the children were given a formal and vocational education – a rare chance at that time.

When the nuns opened the side door of their convent in the morning, they often found babies whose mothers or families left them there out of financial hardship, because of the shame of an unwanted pregnancy or because they were ill. Sometimes they were also left there because the parents believed that the birth of a girl in the year of the tiger brought misfortune. But at least the parents knew that there was the hope of life behind this door. And so the door became Singapore's baby hatch, and was named the 'Gate of Hope'. The number of foundling babies became so great that for a quarter of a century from 1970 there was a separate home for them.

Today the situation is completely different. Singapore is growing too old, and desperately needs children. Llike in many other places, long and expensive periods of training and education mean that people start families later. Many families calculate quite precisely what a child with the best possible education would cost them. State programmes have been created to raise the birthrate. Young academics in particular are given incentives to have children and preferably several of them. Childcare provision with nurseries is comprehensive and exemplary. Posters of the assistance programmes for pregnant teenagers hang at bus stops.

CHIJMES is now a place for restaurants and bars. But the door is preserved as a memorial of the many lives saved here.

Address CHIJMES, 30 Victoria Street, Singapore 187996 (Colonial District) | Getting there MRT to NS 25/EW 13 City Hall or CC 2 Bras Basah | Hours Only viewable from the outside | Tip Lunch in the Asia Grand Restaurant in the Odeon Towers: the Peking duck is a favourite, not only for the many business people here.

# 31 The Gate to Knowledge
*Three arches, one thought*

Those who stepped through this gate in the 1950s knew that their special hour had struck. The three arches stand there, ivory-coloured, massive, tall, dignified and protected by green roof tiles. A humbling stone symbol. The year 1955 stands out clearly above the middle arch.

That was the year that Nanyang Univeristy (Nantah for short, from the Chinese) opened. Its first students had to walk through this gate on their way to the teaching building. Many students followed year upon year. Every morning the gate reminded them to act with dignity and reverence – they were the first to study in the young city state and were to be made aware of the magnitude of their duty.

The three arches symbolise the three elements of traditional Chinese philosophy: *tian* represents the sky, *di* the earth and *ren* humanity and civilisation. But that is not all. The three arches also evoke the three qualities that the students should obtain through hard work and concentration, in order to later form the city state's elite: *cai* urges wisdom in the guiding of the state. *Chang cai* symbolises the ability to do trade and business. And *qing cai* covers the ethics of a person.

Nantah merged in 1980 with the Univeristy of Singapore, becoming a predecessor to the now highly regarded Nanyang Technological University (NTU). The gate that was still reminding students to be humble in the middle of last century didn't really have a place any more in this period of change. Today it stands isolated and almost forgotten in a small park by a housing estate. But because it was testimony to the earlier Singaporean society and the immigrant Hokkien Chinese with their hunger for education and their diligence, there is a replica of it in NTU's Yunnan Garden. It was constructed in front of the former – and beautiful – Nantah library and the old university administration building in 1995.

1955

南洋大學

Address Jurong West Street 93, Singapore 642987 (Jurong) | Getting there MRT to EW 28 Pioneer, then by foot or taxi to Yunnan Park | Hours Always accessible | Tip Jurong Bird Park, the biggest of its kind in Asia, is a paradise for bird lovers (Singaporean wildlife park attractions at www.wrs.com.sg).

# 32 __ Glass Dragons

*Night work for floral splendour*

What happens here above the ground delights tourists and Singaporeans alike. A sea of flowers, never-seen plants from the north-west of the planet, cooled conservatories of unknown proportions. But not many know what goes on behind the scenes of Singapore's huge Gardens by the Bay. The work either takes place at night or underground.

The stunning conservatories in the city's new botanic garden look like two sleeping dragons made of glass. The Flower Dome bulges 38 metres up into the air; the Cloud Forest next to it, with its artificial hill, rises 58 metres. The dome of the first is made of 3,300 glass panels, the other is made using more than 2,500 – which were incidentally designed in Germany. The glass roofs shimmering in the tropical sun are washed thoroughly three times a year.

Only through this do the main characters here come into full bloom. The gardens comprise a total of around 1.5 million plants, all of which require meticulous care and tending.

In a private, air-conditioned flower test centre, gardeners test new plants and breed hybrids. The domes are replanted around seven times a year. This happens overnight, from nine in the evening, when the two houses are closed. Then the hard work begins and continues until three in the morning.

Since they opened in 2012, almost 40 million guests have also been fascinated by 18 enormous artificial trees. The trees have even become an advertising motif of Deutsche Bank. Upon them grow 163,000 hanging plants that were selected from more than 200 species. But the real purpose of the up-to-50-metre-tall steel towers remains hidden: some of the 'Supertrees' serve as chimneys. Deep under the gardens is an incineration plant that produces electricity from green waste – not only from the gardens, but from the whole of Singapore. This is used to cool the greenhouses. And the ashes serve as fertiliser.

Address Gardens by the Bay, 18 Marina Gardens Drive, Singapore 018953 (Marina Bay) | Getting there MRT to CC1/DT16 Bayfront | Hours The conservatories: daily 9am–9pm; outdoor gardens: daily 5–2am | Tip The handmade dumplings in Din Tai Fung in Marina Bay Sands are worth a Michelin star. The kitchen is behind glass so you can watch them being made.

# 33__ The Golden Roof
## An awning for the National Gallery

Sitting on a plastic chair on the lawn of the Padang, sweating in the blazing heat, unshaded from the tropical midday sun – that's how the architect Jean François Milou found his inspiration. The aim was to win a competition, to bring together the Supreme Court and the City Hall to create a new national gallery. The French architect experienced at first hand, during his working session in the heat on the lawn in front of the two buildings, the importance that shade has in the tropics: a roof was needed.

Milou won the tender with this roof – a roof unlike any other roof that has gone before. A light canopy made of 15,000 gold-coloured aluminium plates, with cutouts in the most diverse of forms. The interplay of light and shade thus became the central theme of Milou's construction. His roof is the connecting element between the separate buildings: the perforated plates filter the dazzling light of the tropical sun and transform it into airy gold. Spots of sun and shadowy effects alternate, as under the palm-leaf roof of a hut.

The fleece stretches over both roofs and spans the entrance portal – shining golden, still visible from the other end of the Padang, where Milou once had his brainwave in the midday sun. This awning appears very Asian, but at the same time also very French. Anyone who has walked through Singapore knows the image of colourfully printed awnings protecting shops and their displays from the sun and dust. And what would a typical French street café be without its awning?

Milou continues the subtlety with which he plays with Western and Eastern cultures with the canopy throughout the entire complex: he has carefully united the old colonial elements with the most modern of museum technology and architecture. Thanks to the Frenchman and his perspiration, the National Gallery with its Southeast Asian art is worth its weight in gold.

Address 1 St Andrew's Road, Singapore 178957 (Colonial District) | Getting there MRT to EW 13/NS 25 City Hall | Hours Sat–Thu 10am–7pm, Fri 10am–9pm, tours at www.nationalgallery.sg | Tip On the Padang, the public area in front of the gallery, is the picturesque, colonial-style Singapore Cricket Club from 1852.

# 34 The Good Shepherd
*A time capsule under the bell tower*

For years this cathedral, the oldest Roman Catholic church in Singapore, and simultaneously the seat of its bishop, was only prevented from collapsing by braces. The beige-brown paint was flaking off too – and this despite the fact that the house of worship from 1843 stands in the middle of the kempt Colonial District, next to the shiny Singapore Management University.

However, the costly renovation proved itself to be a stroke of luck, as the builders unearthed ceremonial objects that seemed to be waiting patiently to be rediscovered in forgotten corners of the interior. The greatest wonder of them all was hidden by the collapsed corner column of the portico under the bell tower: a time capsule. Here, under the foundation stone, Jean-Marie Beurel, the father of the French Catholic Mission, together with several members of the congregation, had buried Portuguese, Singaporean and Spanish coins in pharmacy bottles on 18 June, 1843. The offering was meant as a symbol for the conciliation of rival Catholic factions. International Catholic newspapers from that year and the little ceremony book from the first service were also found. They were intended to prove to future generations that the congregation was cultivated and civilised and fostered international communication.

Father Beurel was not only one of the founders of this church. The active clergyman also founded the St Joseph Institute across the road in 1852, a school for boys, which has long since housed the Singapore Art Museum. Two years later, Beurel founded the Convent of the Holy Infant Jesus for the Christian upbringing of girls. Now named CHIJMES, the former convent is home to a lively array of pubs and restaurants.

Today the Good Shepherd is finally pristine again, and all of the exalted artefacts can be admired in the Cathedral Heritage Gallery of the JM Beurel Centre.

Address 'A' Queen Street, Singapore 188533 (Colonial District) | Getting there MRT to CC2 Bras Basah | Hours Mon–Fri 8am–9pm, Sat & Sun 7am–9pm; Heritage Gallery: daily 9am–10pm | Tip Next door is the city's statement on its future: the Singapore Management University. The campus is designed to be highly accessible, and is a very good window on the tertiary education system in Singapore.

# 35__ Goodwood Park Hotel
### *The abrupt end of German comfort*

The little castle sits on a hill in the middle of the city-centre hustle and bustle as if it were from another time. If it could talk, the Goodwood Park Hotel would have many stories to tell. While plantation owners were still cultivating their nutmeg here at the end of the 19th century, the Germans felt an urge to create a piece of home in the tropical heat. The result? The Teutonia Club, with little towers and a roof like a castle on a rocky outcrop overlooking the Rhine. The author David Brazil later jibed that it was the 'only roof in Singapore that would withstand a snow storm'.

It has never snowed in the tropical metropolis – the Teutonia Club became a victim of the political, rather than climatic, turmoil. In World War I the British arrested the one hundred or so Germans on the island and pocketed their sport and recreation club.

After the end of the war it was then auctioned off. The three Manasseh brothers or their representatives raised their hands at the right time. The Sephardic Jews from Calcutta had become super rich through trading opium and rice, and the real estate business. At the time, Ezekiel Saleh Manasseh lived in what is now the British High Commission, Eden Hall. He created Goodwood Hall, an entertainment club with restaurant, out of the former Teutonia building.

The dancing ended in 1942, when the occupying Japanese quartered their officers here. Manasseh died in Japanese custody; his stepson Vivian Bath was taken off to a labour camp on Hokkaido. From there he ended up in Australia and in 1947 he bought his two step-uncles' shares in the Goodwood Park for $600,000 – in order to put it in competition with Raffles Hotel. For this the venerable Goodwood needed to lay some premieres down: it was the first hotel in Singapore with a swimming pool, the first with a refrigerated wine cellar and the first to employ chambermaids.

Address 22 Scotts Road, Singapore 228221 (Centre) | Getting there MRT to NS 22 Orchard | Hours In operation as a hotel | Tip Opposite, in a picturesque black and white house, is the restaurant The Song of India with exquisite Indian cuisine.

# 36 __ The Green Roofs of Tangs
*The doors stay closed at Christmas*

Orchard Road has long denied its Chinese background – if it weren't for the huge pagoda tower with its green roofs and red columns. Today this building is home to the Marriott Hotel. But underneath it is a very special department store: Tangs.

Its architectural style is based on the Palace of Heavenly Peace in Beijing's Forbidden City. As such it stands in sharp contrast to the department store icon ION opposite with its organic-shaped, stainless-steel frontage. Together they form the doorway to Orchard Road.

It is hard to imagine today, but when C. K. Tang, later to become the department store king, bought his piece of land here in 1958, he demonstrated visionary powers: at the time, Orchard Road was still outside the city centre – life played out in the Colonial District. Tang foresaw that it would one day become the heart of the growing metropolis.

He had always been a visionary. When he arrived from China in 1923 he had nothing more than two chests of embroidered tablecloths and bed sheets as merchandise with him. He sold them door to door to the wealthy colonial rulers in Tanglin and Bukit Timah.

His credo remains the philosophy of the department store to this day: honesty, integrity and good value for money. Through this, Tang's business blossomed. By building his shop on Orchard Road, he still reached his old customers, who would drive over this axis into the city centre from the west. In 1975, the old store was pulled down and today's Tang complex was built. The green roofs and red columns known to everyone across the city survived as emblems.

But the department store also became famous due to its owner's faith: C. K. Tang was Christian. And he didn't hide it – his shop stayed closed on Sundays until 1994. At that point he could no longer afford to lose the extra custom and made a compromise: the doors stayed open except for Christmas!

Address 310 Orchard Road, Singapore 238864 (Centre) | Getting there MRT to NS 22 Orchard | Hours Mon–Sat 10.30am–9.30pm, Sun 11am–8.30pm | Tip In the small restaurant Nanbantei (#05-132) in the Far East Plaza next door, you sit cramped together, like in Japan, and eat delicacies cooked on a charcoal grill.

# 37__Harmony in Diversity
*Purely a matter of faith*

No one ends up at this gallery accidentally – you really have to know where you're going. The museum to Singapore's diversity and harmony of faiths is on the fourth floor of the austere Ministry of National Development. It isn't surprising that such a museum is located in a ministry in the city-state – the diversity of faiths and especially the harmony among religions is the basis of the coexistence and of the wealth of Singapore and is therefore also a state affair.

The four exhibition rooms are colourful and full of multimedia exhibits. If you want to interest Singaporeans in a particular theme, you have to define it as clearly as possible, make it interactive and present it well. This has been achieved here. The quantity in itself is surprising: 10 religions – Baha'i, Buddhism, Christianity, Hinduism, Islam, Jainism, Judaism, Sikhism, Taoism and Zoroastrianism – are briefly introduced with their basic messages and some typical exhibits.

Things get really exciting in the next room, where the curators describe religiously motivated, violent clashes in Singapore. From this they bridge the gap to the room in which the peaceful coexistence of the religions in this city is presented: the Loyang Tua Pek Kong temple, in which Buddhists, Hindus, Taoists and Muslims all pray in harmony. Or the hawker centres, in which the foods of the three largest ethnic groups – Chinese, Malay and Indian – must all be represented. Those who eat together don't fight against each other. Or the state-run residential blocks, where all of Singapore's ethnic groups are represented proportionally, so that no ghettos arise.

The small museum calls for respect towards other religions, to secure peace and prosperity. Visitors from Europe may be given cause for contemplation here – this hidden museum offers solutions to some of the most burning issues.

# 38 Harry's Bar

*Of speculators and sipping*

It's not the way that anyone would want to become famous. Nick Leeson was the name of the man who triggered the first big modern financial scandal. He worked at the Barings Bank in Singapore. And sometimes he drank in Harry's Bar on Boat Quay. That made the bar itself famous – even though Leeson himself stated that he spent more time at Big Ben, at the other end of Boat Quay, at the time. The managers of Harry's simply know how to make money from the story of a failed banker.

But first things first. The year is 1995, February to be precise. The British stockbroker Nick Leeson of Barings Bank has amassed losses of more than a billion U.S. dollars over the previous months, but it still doesn't appear to have been noticed by anyone. However, he loses a further 50 million on the morning of the 23rd, when he banks on the Japanese Nikkei Index and its value plummets. Leeson flees the country with his wife, is later arrested in Frankfurt and is extradited to Singapore. Six and a half years of imprisonment in Changi Prison follow.

Leeson was considered a star trader, but wasn't an easy man to be around. He was thrown out of the venerable cricket club after making a racist remark. And he spent his first night in police custody after an alcohol-fuelled argument in a pub.

There is nothing left of the former British traditional bank, which fell victim to its own trader, in Singapore's banking district. But Harry's Bar plays with its memory: a party was thrown here to mark Nick's release from prison, which was given the wonderful title 'Fight of Freedom'. Traders still meet at Harry's at the end of their working day, under the towers of Singapore's huge palaces of finance. Since Leeson's parting they can also partake in a new cocktail – the 'Bank Breaker', a mix of Midori, whiskey and soda, might leave you with a rather bitter aftertaste.

Harry's Cupcakes

## Bank Breaker

A deceptively sweet but potent shot of muskmelon liqueur, whisky and soda water.

Shot | $10.00    Tray of 6 | $50.00

**...kaze**

...efreshing shooter of vodka and ...ntreau flavoured with sweet and sour ...r a pleasant sweetness.

Shot | $10.00    Tray of 6 | $50.00

## Jägerbomb

Get pumped with this tasty sweet sho... jägermeister and red bull. Best enjo... a tray of 6 shooters.

Shot | $10.00    Tray of 6

**...wjob**
...eamy shooter of
...aileys topped

Shot | $10.00

Cupcake

Address 28 Boat Quay, Singapore 049818 (Colonial District) | Getting there MRT to EW 14/NS 26 Raffles Place | Hours Sun–Thu 11.30–1am, Fri & Sat 11.30–2am | Tip If you're head over heels into fun, get yourself to G-Max Reverse Bungee opposite on Clarke Quay . . . on an empty stomach!

# 39__The Helix Bridge
*The DNA of the bridge*

Venice is the city of canals, Singapore the city of bridges. Of pedestrian bridges to be precise. There are apparently 560 of them in the city, but no one knows the exact total. As many of them are covered, they also serve to protect people in the tropical city from the sun and rain. They are a welcome gift of the government to its voters. The cross on your ballot paper may determine whether you cross from the bus stop to the other side of the road with dry feet in the future.

The city is like a museum for pedestrian bridges, and it all began in 1964, the year before independence, with a steel and wood construction over the harbour road, Collyer Quay. This has long since become an enclosed structure, with jewellers and boutiques setting up shop in the middle.

The longest pedestrian bridge over a road measures 145 metres, the shortest is more of a stile. The architects from Mak Ng & Associates built the bridge in Ang Mo Kio in the form of freight containers, with hexagonal cut-out windows. And the oldest has stood on Serangoon Road, unchanged, since 1967.

While diverse in style, the bridges must all adhere to detailed rules: from the type of LED-lighting to the concrete, to the steel for their railings. This must be of the same quality that was also used for the external structure of the Petronas Towers in Malaysia's capital, Kuala Lumpur.

The most striking of the pedestrian bridges spans the end of Marina Bay. The Helix, designed by Australian and Singaporean architects, has four viewing platforms. Opened in 2010, it not only allows pedestrians to walk, it also aims to educate them. It is built like a double helix, and at night the letters 'C', 'G', 'A' and 'T' shine out in red and green in reference to Cytosine, Guanine, Adenine and Thymine, the four bases of DNA and a nightmare for any student struggling with biology.

**Address** Between Marina Centre and Marina South, Singapore 049213 (Marina Bay) | **Getting there** MRT to DT 4/CC 15 Promenade | **Hours** Always accessible | **Tip** In Food Court, Makansutra Gluttons Bay on the left next to the Esplanade, you can sit with a fantastic view of the bay.

# 40 Helmut Newton's Suite

*Black-and-white photographer, colourful love life*

We know the man as a great photographer of great – mostly naked – women. But even the greats start small. It was no different for Helmut Neustädter from Berlin-Schöneberg. The young Jew was forced to flee his sheltered world in 1938. The *Conte Rosso* docked at Singapore harbour just before Christmas, and it was 'as if someone had thrown a boiling hot, damp towel over my face', he – now long since known around the world as Helmut Newton – wrote of the unbearable tropical heat in his memoirs.

The beginning was difficult. 'I had no work, I practically lived off refuge, I saw the boats that arrived from Europe and set off for Europe, and I cried my eyes out.' But the 18-year-old didn't give up. He was helped, if his autobiography is to be believed, by women, who showered him with love, sex and money.

The young Neustädter managed to get a position as a photographer for *The Straits Times*. But because, according to his own accounts, he was so stupid that he 'didn't even end up with any pictures on the film', he was fired after just two weeks. And again it was a woman who bailed him out – this time she came straight from the Singaporean upper class. Josette Fabien spoke fluent English, French and Malay, had painted red finger nails and owned a profitable advertising company. But above all she lived in Raffles Hotel. She also had her office there. Neustädter wouldn't have been Newton if it had taken long before the two became lovers under the 'snow-white mosquito net' in a suite of the Raffles Hotel.

In 1940, with the advent of World War II, the stateless photographer was sent to an Australian internment camp as an 'enemy alien'. By then, he had already mastered further amorous adventures and the setting up of his own atelier. He summed up the city that had helped him on his feet in this way: 'A first-class city for second-class people.'

Address Raffles Hotel, 1 Beach Road, Singapore 189673 (Colonial District) | Getting there MRT to NS 25/EW 13 City Hall | Hours The hotel and the hotel arcade will reopen in the second half of 2018 after their complete renovation. | Tip Norman Foster's most recent architectural project – an interplay of restored colonial buildings and ultramodern skyscrapers – is the South Beach complex opposite the Raffles.

# 41___ The Hotel Guards
## *The fight for guests*

An Indian Sikh stands in front of the world-famous Raffles Hotel as its doorman. Not only does he allocate parking spaces for guests' cars, he serves, almost more importantly, as a photo motif for the many tourists.

Two very different figures stand in front of the Hilton Hotel on Orchard Road: their expressions are gloomy, they are larger than life and dark. They are two Chinese generals from ancient times, guarding the sleep of the guests. Wei Chi Jing De and Qin Sho Bao are for the Chinese the best two to guard entryways and gates. In real life they served the abominable emperor Tang Tai Zong. He had problems sleeping – which isn't much of a surprise as he secured his rule by massacring his opponents – so he consulted two of his high-ranking warriors. They promised to guard the gate to his palace personally and to ward off any unwelcome intruders and evil spirits. The emperor slept peacefully from then on.

That's what the American hotel chain must have wished for their guests when they commissioned the two clay figures in 1975. The Chinese-Malaysian potter Aw Eng-Kwang took the order for the 2.7-metre-tall guards with their weapons and armour very seriously, first needing to build a kiln big enough to fire the bearded warriors in one piece. Eight workers needed half a year just to create their moulds. In the end they seemed to have created a world record: never before had such large figures been fired as the two fierce warriors – but this is doubtful.

In the first years the two warriors stood in the lobby of the Hilton, but they must have frightened the guests so much that they had to be moved outside in 1981, into the flower beds on Orchard Road. That is where they have stood to this day, swinging swords and cracking whips against the traffic, a Häagen-Dazs ice-cream stall in between them. Guests enter the Hilton behind their backs …

Address 581 Orchard Road, Singapore 238883 (Centre) | Getting there MRT to NS 22 Orchard | Tip Sitting drinking a beer under birch trees on Orchard Road? A couple of Germans have found happiness with their burger bar Hans im Glück (hansimglueck-burgergrill.sg).

# 42___ The Hot Spring
*Don't get cold feet*

Drifting on your back in hot water. Splashing around under tropical skies. Counting the stars while lying on top of gentle waves: Asia, the region of hot springs. But not in Singapore. Sure, there are plenty of expensive spas here. But the state, which otherwise taps every possible source of money-making, had almost overlooked the treasure it possesses in Sembawang.

Singapore's hot spring bubbles away in a hard-to-get-to location on the edge of the city. A concrete path leads through a prohibited military zone, marked off by wire-mesh fencing. You may start thinking of turning back, but suddenly there it is: the spring. The hot water comes out of a rusty hydrant that is embedded in an aged concrete slab at 70 degrees Centigrade. A couple of worn-out plastic chairs stand next to the fence, for the few locals who wash here and fill up their plastic canisters with the valuable water. Some immerse eggs in it.

Many here believe that the water has healing properties. It is, in fact, rich in chlorine and sulphur, which your nose will confirm without mistake.

The hot springs were discovered by a Chinese businessman in Kampong Ayer Panas, Malay for 'hot water village', in 1909. He bottled the water and sold it. In the 1920s, a drinks company took over the business, which has long since been discontinued. Only the Japanese occupiers in World War II recognised the treasure: bathing in hot water is a central part of life for the virtually bathing-addicted Japanese. That is why they built bathhouses here – but these have completely disappeared.

After decades of discussion there are now ideas afoot to market the liquid treasure. They may open a national hot spring park. However, there are also those who want the spring to be left as rustic as it is now – with its hydrant, concrete slab and plastic chairs. The water will be the same either way.

Address Gambas Avenue, Singapore 737753 (Sembawang) | Getting there MRT to NS 11 Sembawang, then bus 859 to Block 114 Sembawang Road, then 10-minute walk | Hours Daily 7am–7pm | Tip White Restaurant (22 Jalan Tampang), which used to be called Sembawang White Beehoon, is a local celebrity that guests are prepared to travel a long way to get to.

# 43___Ice-Cream Uncles

*Eat sweet, do good!*

Strange, overloaded vehicles circle through in the city traffic mornings and evenings. Whether they are bicycles or motorbikes, they always have colourful Wall's or Magnolia boxes strapped on the back and at the front, all around the rider, and on the side a carefully secured, folded parasol.

The ice-cream sellers are out and about. They are the last representatives of the fraternity of street traders who used to hawk their food all over Singapore. All other mobile food stalls have long since been banished to the hawker centres or food courts. But the ice-cream sellers have remained. With the corresponding emotion attached, they are affectionately called 'ice-cream uncles' by Singaporeans, a sweet memory of childhood.

Once they stop on the pavement on Orchard Road and open up their colourful parasols, they are soon surrounded by a cluster of people. They sell an ice cream typical for Singapore: a block of ice cream, at least thumb-thick, is stuffed between two rectangular wafers or, even more popular, wrapped inside a folded, multicoloured, floppy slice of bread. It's then wrapped in paper and eaten from the hand – delicious. It's basically an ice-cream sandwich.

But the various flavours on offer are very unique. The ice-cream uncles do sell chocolate, vanilla and raspberry, but in Singapore there is also durian and sweetcorn, peppermint and coconut.

The uncles are mostly older men, many of them long past retirement age. They improve their income with this relatively easy-going work. Just like many of the old taxi drivers, who squint with exertion over the steering wheel. Or the paper collectors, pushing their carts through the streets of Chinatown or Tiong Bahru. Singapore does offer everyone a state-subsidised apartment, but many old people hardly have enough for their daily needs. So make sure you eat lots of ice cream!

**Address** In front of the Takashimaya department store complex on the corner of Orchard Road and Bideford Road, Singapore 238873 (Centre) | **Getting there** MRT to NS 22 Orchard | **Tip** In Japan Food Town on the 4th floor of the Wisma Atria department store, numerous restaurants offer all kinds of food options from sushi to yakitori.

# 44 Indian National Army Marker

*The forgotten army*

The 1940s were wild years for the city. The Japanese had Singapore in their brutal grip. For the Indian liberation movement, the city became the starting point for their struggle against British colonialism at home.

Subhas Chandra Bose, leader of the Indian National Congress and of the independence movement, wanted, unlike other members of his party, Mahatma Gandhi and Jawaharlal Nehru, to use weapons to oust the British from India. He attempted to make ties with the Nazis in Berlin, while rejecting their racial laws. At the end of October 1943, in a crowded Cathay cinema in Singapore, Bose declared the foundation of the Provisional Government of Free India. He built up the Indian National Army, with support in the form of vast sums of money from Indians living in Southeast Asia, and recruited young fighters. The hymn by Nobel Prize for Literature-winner Rabindranath Tagore, 'Jana Gana Mana', now India's national anthem, became the battle song of the Bose troops, 'faith', 'unity' and 'sacrifice' being its catchwords. Bose had them engraved into a memorial, which he dedicated in the summer of 1945 near today's Esplanade concert hall. On the orders of Lord Mountbatten, who oversaw the return of Singapore to the British, it was immediately torn down after the war. Bose's plan of attacking the British in India from the east, via Burma, side by side with Japanese soldiers, failed with the Japanese defeat.

In August 1945, Bose planned to fly from Singapore to Tokyo. He never arrived. His death has been subject to a host of rumours, which range from a crash to him wasting away in a Russian prison camp in Siberia. His stash of jewels, said to value more than four million U.S. dollars, also disappeared. In 1995, half a century after the end of the war, Singapore dedicated 11 war memorials. One of them stands at the location of the former memorial of the Bose troops.

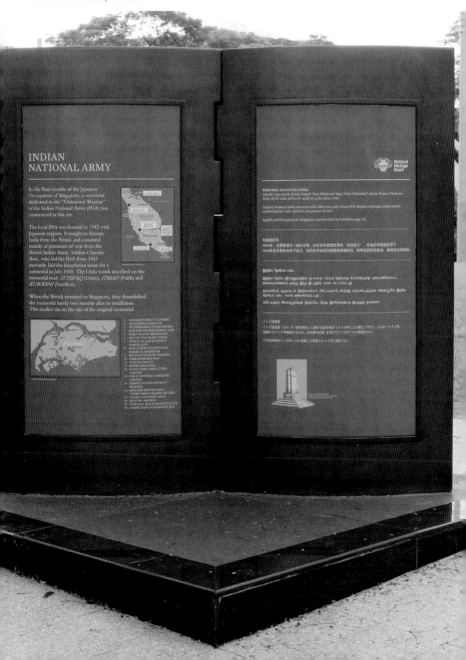

# 45_ The Indian Rubber Tree

*A smoother journey*

He is a giant. Broad-shouldered, powerful, taking up the space he needs. And he has a story to tell, not only because he is already more than 60 years old.

The foundation of the wealth of this island was its plantations, which were created in the middle of the 19th century by the active British with their labourers, in the jungle beyond today's Orchard Road. The colonial rulers began trading in rubber from very early on. The Indian rubber tree grew in the jungle of southern Asia and was now cultivated. Workers from Malaya to Ceylon boiled its juice into *gutta rambong*, a red-brown, rubber-like material.

The end of the tree was nigh, when the director of the Botanic Gardens at the time, Sir Henry Nicholas Ridley, began cultivating the para rubber tree from the Amazon region, the latex of which was considered to be of better quality. It was also a more efficient tree, able to be cut and milked after six years. With the Indian rubber tree the wait was at least 15 years.

Therefore the tall Indian rubber trees soon became obsolete. But without these trees, the city may never have become what it is. That's why the tree on the side wing of the Singaporean National Museum and those of the same species throughout the tropical metropolis are now protected.

In any case, the slower-growing giant is the more beautiful of the two: it can reach a good 30 metres in height and its aerial roots then form an impenetrable meshwork that push back into the ground. In the case of the tree in front of the museum, they have even grown over an old white iron fence that once marked off the site. It can already be seen growing here on photos from the middle of the 1950s. And because it grows so long and tall and free, the Indian rubber tree in front of the museum is also part of a tree route, that the authorities signpost right through the old town.

Address Next to the National Museum of Singapore, 93 Stamford Road, Singapore 178897 (Colonial District) | Getting there MRT to CC 2 Bras Basah | Tip The National Museum has a classical facade, but is very modern on the inside, just like the excellent exhibitions, not only on national history.

# 46 — The Istana Kampong Glam
*The lucrative intelligence of the 'orangutan'*

It is a handsome palace and a beautiful museum. But the Istana Kampong Glam is also the heart of the city. Without Kampong Glam there would never have been modern Singapore.

The first resident was Sultan Hussein Shah, who had been installed by the British as ruler in February 1819 in order to sign a treaty allowing British manufacturing and trade in Singapore. In 1897, the property was granted to the British colony, although the sultan's descendants were allowed to continue living there, and were given an annual stipend limited to $250,000 in the early 20th century. Hussein has been depicted as an extremely unpleasant fellow. He was summarised by a European man as a fatso, who didn't even have 'the intelligence of an orangutan'.

While the Sultan had initially lived in a wooden house on stilts, his son, Mohammed Ali, had the stone house we see today built in 1843, in a mixture of European colonial style and Malay tradition. Apparently it was designed by the British architect George D. Coleman. Academics believe that the entire quarter, including the large mosques with their golden domes, was laid out according to the rules of an ancient mandala of Buddhist tradition. That didn't concern the British: in order to restrict the power of the sultans, they cut roads right through the quarter. In 1999, the last descendents living on the grounds were relocated in exchange for compensation, and in 2005 the government transformed the palace into the Malay Heritage Centre.

And Sultan Hussein's heirs? Some protested against the new use of 'their palace', but to no avail. They will continue to share the payout from the state for a few more years yet. But as one of the sons of the seventh generation explained: 'We have long since become normal Singaporeans. We do military service and work like everyone else. And some of us even live in subsidised apartments.'

Address 85 Sultan Gate, Singapore 198501 (Kampong Glam) | **Getting there** MRT to EW 12/DT 14 Bugis | **Hours** Tue – Sun 10am – 6pm | **Tip** On the corner of North Bridge Road and Arab Street, an old man crouches under one of the last extendable house ladders, where he runs a tiny shop selling daily essentials, just like many generations before him.

# 47 Jamal Kazura Aromatics
*A thousand and one scents*

Women all around the world love perfumes. They are particularly helpful when the climate is hot. While all the big names of the international world of fragrances are represented in the city's department stores, a very unique perfume sector has developed in Singapore's Muslim quarter. A couple of shops here specialise in perfume oils, fragrances composed without the use of alcohol. This way the perfumers in the tropical metropolis' Little Arabia can satisfy their Muslim customers.

Jamal Kazura Aromatics is the prettiest of these shops. When you enter you are almost blown away by a symphony of fragrances. In the next moment you will see the seemingly endless number and variety of flacons on the shelves along the mirrored wall, some full, some still empty. You can, of course, buy fragrance creations, pre-produced and bottled by Jamal Kazura and his son. The bestseller is 'Raja Jasmin'. Others include all the popular international perfumes, but in perfume oil form. But it gets better: on request the perfumers from Jamal Kazura will also mix a completely individual fragrance oil for each customer.

You can chose from a variety of oils such as ginger and nutmeg from Indonesia, geranium from China, jasmine from Egypt, saffron from Spain, rose from Bulgaria, sandalwood from India or frankincense from Yemen and Oman. Jamal Kazura still finds it fascinating to see which fragrance composition his customers ultimately choose. 'A fragrance is like music, some people like rock, others love classical or jazz,' he says.

And then he adds that lighter scents are now popular, not the heavier ones like in the past. His son is building up this modern, lighter segment. And Kazura Junior has something for the very young too: scents that smell of food, like strawberries, chocolate or ice cream.

Address 728 North Bridge Road, Singapore 198696 (Kampong Glam) | Getting there MRT to EW 12/DT 14 Bugis | Hours Daily 9am–6pm | Tip The residents of the quarter like to sit at 21 Baghdad Street, where the authentic teh tarik, 'pulled' tea with milk, is served.

# 48__ The Japanese Cemetery
*Hope for lost souls*

This place is enveloped by silence. Not only the cemetery itself, but also the area around it. Japanese soldiers who died during the occupation are among those buried here and no one wants to stir up the feelings of the older generation of Singaporeans who suffered under them.

The cemetery has a unique history. In 1891, the three brothel owners Futaki Takajiro, Shibuya Ginji and Nakagawa Kikuzo received permission from the colonial government to bury dead prostitutes. They chose a corner of their rubber plantation. In thanks for their good deed, two large rubber trees have stood in the graveyard to this day. In those days most of the *karayuki-san*, the prostitutes of the harbour city, came from Japan. They are buried in about half of the thousand or so graves here.

After the capitulation in 1944, soldiers of the occupation who committed suicide or were executed due to their crimes were also buried here.

But there are also graves in the cemetery of Japanese people who are well-known, at least in their own circles: Kantaro Ueyama, the son of the inventor of the smoke spiral for keeping away mosquitos, who died in a plane crash in Sembawang. Or Futabatei Shimei – he is cited in the encyclopaedias as the founder of realism in Japanese literature. He was working as a newspaper correspondent and was on a return journey from Russia when he died in Singapore in 1909.

Since 1969 the cemetery park has belonged to the Japanese Association, and the last funeral here took place in 1973. The park is wonderfully well-kept, and that is thanks to an international friendship. The vigil over the dead, over victims and offenders, is kept by Singaporean Lim Geok Qi, who took over the role from his father. He knows them, the stories of the poor and lost, the murderers and those who left their homes for this foreign land with grand ambitions, but lost their lives here.

Address 825B Chuan Hoe Avenue, Singapore 549853 (Hougang) | Getting there MRT to NE 14 Hougang, then bus 116 or 147 to After Serangoon North Avenue 1, then five-minute walk | Hours Daily 8am – 6.30pm | Tip At Just Anthony, in an old villa with a warehouse at 379 Upper Paya Lebar Road, you can still find the odd beautiful piece of furniture or decoration.

# 49 Jurong Eco-Garden
*The green bridge*

These scientists certainly have it cushy. Those researching transportation concepts or racking their brains over energy networks in the Eco-Campus of the Nanyang Technological University are working on the future. The state therefore makes sure they have the best conditions in which to do so. This includes a park that starts just behind the labs.

The Jurong Eco-Garden, on the far west of the island, is the city's least well known botanical garden. Tourists simply don't come here, which is a shame as the park is refined and wild in equal measure. There are signs all over warning of wild boars and monkeys. A stream meanders along the path and flows into artificial lakes. The green grounds, measuring almost five hectares, appear tidy, but interventions in nature are limited to what is necessary. For example there is an artificial stone ramp made out of recycled material on the lookout hill. There is a compost corner and an ecological toilet. So the green heart of the researcher beats a little faster when they spend their lunch breaks here.

The most remarkable achievement of the garden is the connection between new and old: its paths wind around Singapore's two ancient dragon kilns, the Thow Kwang Kiln (see ch. 102) and the Guan Huat Kiln, and their ponds. In this way the park connects Singapore's pottery tradition with the spearhead of the sciences seeking to secure the city's future. This is also reflected in the sculptures dotted around the park: *Sculpted Maze* was fired in Thow Kwang Kiln at 1,280 degrees and made of clay amassed from the excavation of the university building. *Another Way to Perceive the Rain of the Forest* was hewn from basalt boulders that were removed to construct the oil-storage caverns under Jurong Island. This green lung thus forms a bridge between yesterday and tomorrow in a city so young that it is still fighting to create its own history.

Address 1 Cleantech Loop, Singapore 637141 (Jurong) | Getting there MRT to EW 27 Boon Lay, then bus 199 to Before Nanyang Avenue | Hours Always accessible | Tip Worth a look: the test cars for Singapore's research programme into self-driving cars are parked in front of the Cleantech building.

# 50__Jurong Fishery Port
*The early bird catches the fish*

Can't sleep? But you already know all of the best bars and your high heels are blistering your feet anyway? Then slip into your flip-flops and head on down to the fish market.

At Jurong Fishery Port, the oldest and largest fish market in Singapore, things already start heating up around midnight, it's at its busiest between three and four in the morning, by around six all of the business has been done and the market closes.

Here the fish trade is still authentic, as the boats land their fish here and the buyers check the goods. This is the place for large-scale buyers for the supermarket chains, fish traders from wet markets and restaurant chefs alike. You can watch the professionals at it: for them the market is a place of work, not recreation. Of course, the freshly caught product here is around 20 per cent cheaper than in the markets of the city.

Most of the fish are carried into the market hall straight from the boats in white polystyrene boxes, and are so fresh that some of them still flounder. But because of the tropical heat, most are laid on ice. That of course melts with time. And so over the course of the early morning the hall becomes flooded with water, and the smells become stronger. By now the puddles have become pools and eventually you're standing ankle-deep in the water in your flip-flops. But the courageous will be rewarded with the sight of the creatures of the sea: baskets full of squid, crab, mackerel, shark, pomfret, parrotfish and mussels, to name but a few.

When it's finally time for a coffee, there is always the adjoining coffee shop. They do, of course, also serve fried fish – freshly bought next door. There have long been plans to open restaurants at the market. Then it will become like Fishermen's Wharf in San Francisco or Tsukiji market in Tokyo. So now is definitely the time for an all-nighter, while you still can…

Address 35 Fishery Port Road, Singapore 619742 (Jurong) | Getting there MRT to EW 26 Lakeside, then by taxi | Hours Tue – Sun 0.30 – 5.30am | Tip The Chinese and the Japanese Garden at Jurong Lake are picturesque and contain bonsai treasures, stone pagodas and tea houses.

# 51 Jurong Town Hall
*For whom the bell tolls…*

Singapore, the small island, need symbols to accompany and promote its growth. The most powerful is Jurong Town Hall. Here, the industrialisation is cast in concrete. At first, and indeed second, glance, the massive white building is reminiscent of the starship *Enterprise*. It has landed on an elevation in the middle of Jurong.

This suburb is the symbol of the rapid development of the city state. The Jurong Town Corporation, JTC for short, was formed in 1968 and has been responsible for the building and running of industrial facilities in Singapore to this day. What may sound boring is the foundation of the city. JTC runs industrial sites, but most recently has also created subterranean oil caverns equipped with the most modern of technology.

One year after the foundation of JTC, the city began looking for an appropriate home for its development agency. What is now highly developed industrial land around Jurong was a wasteland at the time, with fish and crab farms along the coast. But the angular, inwardly drawn administration building grew here by 1974, an icon of the development ahead. The modernist building stands for rationality and efficiency. It comprises 27,000 square metres over five storeys. Until JTC moved to a new home in the year 2000, numerous dignitaries had paid their respects to the building, also in order to learn from Singapore's development. Notable names such as Deng Xiaoping, the very-soon-to-be leader of China, and the former general secretary of the United Nations, Kurt Waldheim, planted trees in the garden.

Today it is home to several chambers of commerce. Just like JTC in the early days, they too should increase productivity. To do so it is good to know from the very beginning what the time is: the clock tower, which was Southeast Asia's tallest at the time and is now a protected historic monument, towers over the modernist building.

Address 9 Jurong Town Hall Road, Singapore 609431 (Jurong) | Getting there MRT to EW 24/NS 1 Jurong East | Hours Only viewable from the outside | Tip Interest in science and technology is playfully promoted at Science Centre Singapore with its 850 exhibits and 8 exhibitions.

# 52 Kaya at Chin Mee Chin

*Sweet memories*

You pay a visit to the last 1950s, coffee shop in Katong on a Sunday and you can't get a seat. How can that be?

It certainly can't be due to the furnishings. In the shophouse's plain, plain room, the round teak tables with marble slabs run along the walls on the left and right. In between are refrigerators, the metal cake display cabinet, and at the end a small sink. Practical. And everything is furnished just like it was in 1950 when the Tan family opened their business here.

So is it the *kopi* and the *kaya* toast? This classic Singaporean breakfast consists of *kaya*, a kind of jam made of coconut milk, egg yolk and sugar, seasoned with pandan leaves. This is spread on buttered toast. The bread here is still home baked. With it comes a bowl of half-cooked eggs, which has dark soya sauce mixed in with it. And of course the home-roasted coffee, which is called *kopi*, served in all of the Singaporean variations (see ch. 20).

Or is it because of the croissants filled with cream, custard pastries and cream cakes sitting in the display cabinet and just waiting to be taken out and eaten?

The attraction of the place isn't due to any of the above on their own. It is the combination of it all that awakens Singaporean memories of childhood, of smells and tastes of days gone by. A little bit of home and identity in the middle of a metropolis that no longer sleeps, in amongst all of the city's new, trendy, over-styled designer cafés.

Finally! A free table, between a family with two small children and their grandparents and a table of two teenagers. Opposite is an old married couple, sipping at their coffee in silence. Right in the middle of Katong, the quarter on the East Coast, where there's a good mixture of Singaporeans and expats. They all share a passion for *kopi* and *kaya* and cake. As long as it's being served at Chin Mee Chin.

**Address** Chin Mee Chin Confectionery, 204 East Coast Road, Singapore 428903 (Katong) | **Getting there** MRT to CC 8 Dakota, then bus 10 along East Coast Road to Opposite The Holy Family Church | **Hours** Tue–Sun 8.30am–4pm | **Tip** The Katong Antique House is run by the specialist for Peranakan antiques, Peter Wee. He also offers tours through his original shophouse (+65 63458544).

# 53 Keramat Radin Mas Ayu
*The grave of the golden princess*

Believers still come to this grave deep in the jungle to pay homage to the 'golden princess'. She was the focus and victim of a family drama that took place before the founding of Singapore in the then sultanate, and is revered to this day for her resolute action through love of her father.

Her grave lies at the foot of Mount Faber in what was then the village of Telok Blangah, now a quarter of the same name. The story of Radin Mas Ayu is the story of great love. Initially the love of the parents for one another and then the love of the father for the daughter.

The father was a cosmopolitan Javanese prince and a courageous warrior. He fell in love with a dancer. The couple lived together in secret because of their difference in status and were blessed with a beautiful daughter – the golden princess. When the prince's father found out about this, he had the family's house burned to the ground. The beloved woman died, but the girl was saved by a loyal servant. When the prince heard this news, he broke with his family and went to Telok Blangah with his daughter and the servant. There he lived undetected. But he fought so successfully against pirates that the sultan became aware of him and recognised him. He gave the brave warrior his own daughter's hand in marriage and the pair had a son together.

And so everything would have come to a happy end, if not for the jealousy of the new wife towards the beauty of her stepdaughter and her close relationship to her father. She wanted to marry her stepdaughter off to her nephew, against her will. He abducted the father and threatened to kill him if Radin Mas Ayu wouldn't marry him.

The wedding ceremony ended in scandal: the conspiracy was uncovered. The nephew tried to murder the father but Radin Mas Ayu threw herself in the way of the curved dagger to protect him. The knife struck her right through the heart.

**Address** 10 Mount Faber Road, Singapore 099199 (Telok Blangah) | **Getting there** MRT to NE 1/CC 29 HarbourFront | **Hours** Daily 9am–6pm | **Tip** Very unusual for Singapore is the Old Habits at 38 Telok Blangah Road: the young hosts run a café with an antiques shop.

# 54 Lee Kuan Yew's House

*Small house with explosive power*

The house at 38 Oxley Road – modest by downtown standards – is on golden ground, in the centre of the city. But it hasn't brought its heirs much luck. In fact, it ended up igniting an almost unparalleled inheritance dispute that shook the city to its foundations.

Lee Kuan Yew, the esteemed and almost legendary founding father of modern Singapore who died in 2015, lived in this little house with his family. It was his desire that the house would be torn down after his death so that it wouldn't become a site for hero worship. But things turned out rather different.

In the summer of 2017, a dispute about the future of the house escalated among its three heirs, among them the serving prime minister, Lee Hsien Loong. The explosive part of it: it was carried out publicly, in all its details, via Facebook. First the row ashamed Singaporeans, then it appalled them. Especially because the younger brother made accusations of the older and serving head of government, for which anyone else in Singapore would have been sued into the Stone Age and back. But Prime Minister Lee Hsien Loong tempered justice with mercy and declared that in Chinese families the older brother does not sue the younger brothers. He had long since packed his things and flown to Hong Kong with his wife.

In the end, the small house on Oxley Road became the subject of a comprehensive debate in parliament. There is much to suggest that it could be pronounced a national memorial – or at least its living room could, from which the old Lee commented on the development of half of Asia and sometimes even steered it. In every other country in the world it would have been a decision that would take a few minutes. But Singapore tried to stay restrained, not to run riot, not to display too much self-confidence. Just like the 'Little Red Dot', as it sees itself, in accordance with its position on the map.

Address 38 Oxley Road, Singapore 238629 (Centre) | Getting there MRT to NS 24/ NE 6/CC 1 Dhoby Ghaut | Hours Only viewable from the outside | Tip The Istana, the President's Palace with its large surrounding park, is only open to the public five times a year, on Chinese New Year, Labour Day, Hari Raya Puasa, National Day and Deepavali. Take your chance and go there!

# 55__The Lim Bo Seng Memorial

*The martyr*

The young city is not yet rich in national heroes, but one of them is Lim Bo Seng. It is to him that Singapore has dedicated its only memorial to the fate of an individual survivor of World War II. The 3.6-metre-tall octagonal pagoda in Esplanade Park was inaugurated on 29 June, 1954, exactly 10 years after Lim's death. Lim's widow commissioned the architect Ng Keng Siang to design it and Singaporeans donated a good 50,000 Singapore dollars for its construction.

The pagoda, whose tower is guarded by four bronze lions, commemorates an extremely determined young man, who only lived in the city for a short time. The son of a powerful brick maker – whose bricks were used in the construction of today's Goodwood Park Hotel (see ch. 35), the then Teutonia Club – came to Singapore from Fujian aged 16 years old. Lim was appalled by the invasion of China by the Japanese, collected for the resistance and organised a strike in a Japanese steel mill in Malaysia. He also collaborated with the British secret service against the Japanese infiltration in Singapore.

Lim escaped certain death just hours before the fall of the city in 1942 by fleeing to China. But he returned to the Malay peninsula at the end of 1943 in a submarine from Calcutta, India with kindred spirits, in order to attack the Japanese. But before the underground fighter reached Singapore, Lim was betrayed and fell into their hands in Ipoh. He died aged 35 after enduring three months of torture.

After the liberation, his remains were brought to Singapore and were buried in a state funeral at the MacRitchie Reservoir. The British and Singaporeans revered him equally. His tormentors, two Japanese secret service officers, were later hanged in Changi Prison. The inscription on Lim's pagoda is written in the four official languages of the city state: English, Mandarin Chinese, Malay and Tamil.

**Address** In Esplanade Park along Connaught Drive, Singapore 179682 (Colonial District) | **Getting there** MRT to CC 3 Esplanade | **Hours** Always accessible | **Tip** At Fullerton Waterboat House (3 Fullerton Road) you can eat expensively at 1919 or The Rooftop, or cheaply at Starbucks – the wonderful view is the same from all three.

# 56  MacDonald House

*House of history*

Singapore is a peaceful city. People of various ethnicities and religions live together in harmony here (with some regulatory intervention, mind you). This wasn't always the case. The ups and downs of the city state's young history are under a magnifying glass at MacDonald House, which is near the governmental palace of Istana in the centre of the city.

From the outside the brick building seems weighty, but not intimidating. Built after the end of the war in 1949, it embodied the new start. It was hailed as 'Malaya's first completely air-conditioned office building'. The citizens were astonished, because new technology enabled the temperature to be individually adjusted in each room. 'The system has a cooling capacity that is equivalent to 170 tonnes of ice a day,' reports claimed. The 10-storey MacDonald House became the forerunner of modern building technology in Singapore.

But a few years later the then head office of the Hong Kong and Shanghai Banking Corporation (HSBC) was to be the subject of very different headlines. Between 1963 and 1966, Indonesia sabotaged the merger of Singapore and Malaya that formed Malaysia. On 10 March, 1965, two assailants detonated a bomb in the building's mezzanine; three people lost their lives and more than 30 were injured. Two elite Indonesian soldiers were hanged as murderers. Overnight the building became a memorial to the political development of Southeast Asia and the birth pangs of Singapore's independence in August that year.

The city state overcame them. And MacDonald House, named after the then governor general of Malaya, Malcolm John MacDonald, became the office of Citibank – and thus a symbol of Singapore as an open financial centre. And as if that weren't enough, MacDonald House now belongs to a foreign investor from, of all places, Indonesia. Thus the story comes full circle.

Address 40A Orchard Road, Singapore 238838 (Colonial District) | Getting there MRT to NS 24/NE 6/CC 1 Dhoby Ghaut | Hours Open 24 hours Mon–Fri | Tip Curious Palette at 64 Prinsep Street serves creative waffle and salad variations in a stylish shop house.

# 57 _ The Maids Meeting at ION
*Theatre on the steps*

The city centre always transforms on Sundays. It's not only Singaporeans who flock here to go shopping or for a meal, or, best of all, both. From morning on, legions of domestic helpers also crowd into the inner city because Sunday is their day off. It is estimated that 250,000 of these maids, as they are called here, live in Singapore. Most of them come from the Philippines and Indonesia, some from India, a growing number from Myanmar. In small groups or in pairs, mostly chattering and laughing, they sit together, eat together, meet their friends.

One of their favourite places is in front of the ION Orchard shopping centre. The large steps here form a stage for this piece of theatre, an ideal place for seeing and being seen. All of the maids have put on their Sunday best and done themselves up, some sexy, some plain, but always dressed and made up very carefully. Now the newly bought purchases are taken out of plastic bags and shown around, appraised, given away, swapped or packed away again. The gossip from their families and friends, about other maids or about their employers is also exchanged.

But the maids also complain about money, or rather its constant shortage. It never seems to be enough if you want to meet all the needs of this consumer-oriented city. The schooling of the children, the subsistence of the parents, the demands of the many poor members of the family: all of them expect money from the maids, who live in rich, clean Singapore.

In some cases this can lead to stealing, lies and cheating. Well-off employers all too easily overlook the fact that life here, despite the good provision, is not easy for these women; that there are decent employees, but also exploitative ones; that being separated from children and sometimes husbands over many years is difficult. The maids are left with little choice than to accept it in order to secure their livelihoods.

**Address** The stone steps in front of ION Orchard at the junction of Paterson Road and Orchard Road, Singapore 238801 (Centre) | **Getting there** MRT to NS 22 Orchard | **Hours** Sundays | **Tip** The Heritage Food Trail offers guided tours through Asian delicacies in the food hall in the basement of ION (book at www.ionorchard.com/en/whats-on/events/item/13-local-food-trail.html).

# 58___Marina One

*Ingenhoven builds a closed display window*

Massive. Powerful. All-consuming. That's the effect of Marina One. A block from the outside, playful on the inside. Designed by Dusseldorf architect Christoph Ingenhoven and his team, the complex is a commitment to place, a commitment to the most modern of architecture and a commitment to collaboration between Singapore and its neighbour Malaysia.

Marina One is on land that has been wrested from the sea. In 1960 fewer than 2 million people lived in Singapore; now it is a good 5.6 million. The only solution is to gain land, to build upwards and also downwards in the future. Ingenhoven is the latest in the worldwide line-up of star architects who have ventured forward to Singapore. He found the right clients straight off: 60 per cent of Marina One belongs to the Malaysian sovereign wealth fund Khazanah, 40 per cent to the Singaporean sovereign wealth fund Temasek. The other German shooting star of the scene, Ole Scheeren, had already built his Duo building at the edge of the Arabian quarter (see ch. 23), commissioned by these two. What could go wrong?

But it is also clear that such a building must become a display window. Marina One attempts to do nothing less than embody Singapore's vision of a 'City in a Garden' with its green courtyard. Two office towers, each with a floor area of 175,000 square metres, two 34-storey residential towers and a shopping centre form a small city. A 'biodiversity garden' on several storeys is intended to create its own microclimate. Reconditioned water flows into the toilets, sunshades and special glass hold out the tropical heat, solar panels make use of the rays. Cyclists will find parking spaces, drivers of electric cars charging stations and subway passengers access to four of the city's six subway lines. For those who can afford it, life in Marina One is good – no matter how closed-off the building may appear from the outside.

Address 21–23 Marina Way, Singapore 018978 (Central Business District) | Getting there MRT to DT 17 Downtown | Hours The 'green heart' garden in the middle of the building with its hanging garden is open 24 hours. | Tip At LeVeL33, the highest microbrewery in the world, according to its own blurb, there is not only fresh draught beer, but also a fantastic view of Marina Bay through ceiling-high panorama windows (level33.com.sg).

# 59___MAS Gallery
*Driving Singapore to ruin*

You don't like Singapore? The city really gets on your nerves? It's too loud, and then on top of all that it rains too? You are fed up, yes, even angry, and really want to show Singapore how you feel? Well there is a place for you too: the gallery at the Monetary Authority of Singapore. Here you can really drive Singapore to financial ruin.

Digitally of course. On a computer in the highly modern MAS Gallery, you will be promoted to become boss of the city state's central bank. And thus you can make all the financial-political decisions. Sounds dull? It isn't! You immediately see what happens when you meddle with the virtual interest rates on the screen: more unemployment, higher prices, vacant apartments. Basically all the things that Singapore is trying to avoid with all its might.

Steering the country clear of all this in real life is the Monetary Authority of Singapore's job. It is made up of the city's best civil servants, supervised by the minister of finance. Their task is not only – like most central bankers in the West – to keep inflation within a defined bracket. It is also active in ensuring that the rich tropical island can continue to grow. MAS is a politically led central bank that covers a large scope of duties.

It has done this so well thus far that it has gifted itself a small museum. Opposite are the rooms of Reflections@MAS, where the agency celebrates its staff and its top executives. In the museum you can learn what makes central bankers tick. But you also learn how Singapore has become an Asian financial hub. You can identify counterfeit money. And you can get to know the city state's financial system on a big screen.

Admittedly, this isn't everyone's idea of a holiday activity. But if it's raining and if you really want to understand how this city got to where it is today, then an hour at the MAS Gallery is worth investing.

Address 10 Shenton Way, Singapore 079117 (Central Business District) | Getting there MRT to EW 15 Tanjong Pagar | Hours Mon–Fri 9.30am–5.30pm, Sat 9.30am–1.30pm | Tip Take some time to browse and discover new books at Littered with Books, 20 Duxton Road.

# 60 __ The Masonic Hall

*Open behind closed doors*

A rich cosmopolitan city like Singapore must be open. So open, that members-only clubs certainly have a right to exist. The Falun Gong sect is allowed to practise here, while it is persecuted in China. There are multiple representatives of the Rotary and Lions Club. There is the Club of Millionaires. There are the Chinese clans. And private 'lifestyle clubs', such as the Goh Loo Club, 1880 or Madison Rooms, spring up time and again – offering privileges for high membership fees.

But the oldest private association in the city must be the Freemasons lodge Zetland in the East No. 748 (now renumbered as 508). It was initiated on 26 February, 1845. The Freemasons, who can be traced back to the 16th century in England, had taken root in the British colony. Hardly a great surprise, as the founder of the city of Singapore, Sir Stamford Raffles, was himself a Freemason. The first member in Singapore was the lawyer William Napier (Napier Road runs through Tanglin). He was later followed by Admiral Henry Keppel (Keppel Road runs along the port), and Attorney General Thomas Braddell (Braddell Road is in Toa Payoh, in the centre of the island).

The lodges have met in the Masonic Hall, a Neoclassical building, which could also house a court, since 1879. It continues to be shrouded in mystery. Sure, there was an open day here in 2002, when the Freemasons gave away cinema tickets to poor children. Seven years later the stone block was also given a new blue-and-white paint job, which made it appear much more friendly. And everyone is welcome to eat at the restaurant too. And yet the Freemasons have a particular attraction here in the tropical metropolis, because, as elsewhere, many of their rituals take place behind closed doors. That said, mystery also appeals to the modern clubs: the exclusive Madison Rooms, which limits membership to 400, meets in the Masonic Hall.

Address 23A Coleman Street, Singapore 179806 (Colonial District) | Getting there MRT to NS 25/EW 13 City Hall | Hours Daily 10am–midnight | Tip A little further on you can turn onto Armenian Street. At number 39 is the Peranakan Museum, a refuge of the mixed culture of the Peranakan, which is unique to Singapore and the other Straits Settlements.

# 61__The Merlion
## on Marina Bay
*Advertising icon or myth?*

The Merlion is of course Singapore's heraldic animal. You can find out everything about him in the various travel guides. Well, almost everything: this large statue has also once graced a pop-up hotel room. During the 2011 Biennale the Japanese designer Tatzu Nishi constructed a bedroom around the white monument.

But it doesn't stop there. Time and again the city's intellectuals grate against what is from their perspective a childish figure marketed by the city's tourism board. For example, the Singaporean science-fiction writer Kevin Martens Wong wrote a story in which the Merlion is anything but nice – it spits water. His Merlions are like dragons, who shoot their foes with streams of deadly water instead of fire, and have razor-sharp claws. The advertisers' lapdog became Wong's beast. 'Everyone was just thinking about how annoying the Merlion is! So I asked myself – why not look at it from a completely different perspective?'

Wong's book isn't an exception – a whole series of authors who play with the mythology of the city state have sprung up in Singapore. An offered alternative to the Merlion is Pontianak – a female vampire who is feared in Malaysia and Indonesia. 'The Pontianak represents a folk tradition, the Merlion is an artificial narrative from the government. Many of us don't trust the Merlion,' says the author Ng Yi-Sheng. By the way, the Pontianak embodies the spirit of a woman who died during pregnancy.

Maybe the photogenic Merlion *is* the preferable version after all that horror? At least its origins are clear: he is a child of independence, from when the city was searching for its own story. In 1963, the manager of the Van Kleef Aquarium at Fort Canning Park, which closed in 1998, drew the sketch, which the Singapore Tourism Board then included in its logo for the 'Lion City'.

Address 1 Fullerton Road, Singapore 049213 (Marina Bay) | Getting there MRT to EW 14/NS 26 Raffles Place | Hours Always | Tip The gate to Asia: the Asian Civilisations Museum opposite on the river mouth is a real treasure trove of Asian art and culture.

# 62  Mount Serapong
*Cannons that don't shoot*

A mountain is, well, a mountain. But not in Singapore. Here, a hill on the island of Sentosa has been elevated to the title of 'Mount Serapong'. The island doesn't have many other areas of high ground left after all. But beyond any fraudulent labelling, this hidden corner of the fun island offers adventure.

At first, you can only see the satellite installations that Singapore built on Sentosa's then outermost tip in 1971. Rather more interesting for those who aren't into telecommunications is the hill itself. Here, behind numerous 'Do not enter' signs, you will find the remains of Fort Serapong. From 1879, the British had erected a fortress here to protect the harbour on the other side of the water. It formed a quartet together with the maritime fortresses Fort Siloso, Fort Connaught and Imbiah Battery.

Alongside casemates and artillery stands, a connecting tunnel and lookout booths, the British also constructed a chapel for the spiritual well-being of their soldiers up here. There are still living quarters right on the side of the road, built in 1936, that have never been renovated. Locals know the place because of the huge military development carried out under the name Cement Hill. The British gave the essential water reservoir a camouflaged cover: a cement dome that was supposed to look like the summit of a hill. It also served as a lookout.

The two heavy cannons were always primed and ready, but never actually fired a single shot in wartime, because the Japanese invaded Singapore by land in 1942. Before they fled, the British blew up the cannons. Two days later the Japanese bombed the hill fortress. What is left behind today are decaying concrete barracks, the rotating platforms for the cannons, rusting steel railings and retaining rings. This is what makes the place so fascinating for photographers and hobby historians alike.

Address Woolwich Road, Singapore 098687 (Sentosa) | Getting there MRT to CC 29/ NE 1 HarbourFront, then Sentosa Express to Beach Station, then bus B to Sentosa Pavilion at Eton House, walk towards Serapong Hill Road | Tip Tired of war? Take some time out, be pampered and eat delicious snacks under palm trees at the peaceful So Spa (30 Allanbrooke Road).

# 63__Mount Vernon Cantonment

*The call of the mountains*

Gurkhas live on the roof of the world, in Nepal. Some are farmers, some help mountain climbers. But the mountain people are famous for their outstanding warriors. And there are some of those on the tropical island too.

The British and the Indians have already taken advantage of the Gurkhas. They were and still are admired by both armies because of their courage, their self-sacrifice and because they can reportedly kill an enemy at a distance of 30 metres with their curved throwing dagger, the khukuri.

In Singapore they are seen as 'the invisible power'. But they aren't all that invisible – with their blue uniforms, wide-brimmed hats and their Land Rovers they have made up their own unit of the Singaporean police since 1949. They replaced a regiment of Indian Sikh warriors. During the – few – disturbances the Gurkhas have proven their loyalty to the Singaporean state.

They often come to the city at the young age of 18 and stay for two decades. You will meet them in their civvies in the Nepalese restaurants in Little India. But they live with their families in a special part of Singapore – closed off to everyone else: Mount Vernon Cantonment is a piece of the Himalayas in the city. Many shops in the neighbouring streets also live from Nepalese custom – including Johnny Gurkha's tattoo shop. He pricks pictures into the skin of the policemen so that they can be identified if they die. The barrack buildings for the 2,000 or so policemen from the mountains are reminiscent, thanks to their little towers, of Himalayan architecture. Behind the fence, which is impenetrable for outsiders, there are temples, shops and schools. And so that everyone knows just where they are, the road that leads into the quarter is called Kathmandu Road, after the capital of Nepal.

**Address** Along Mount Vernon Road, Singapore 539247 (Paya Lebar) | Getting there MRT to NE 11 Woodleigh, then bus 100 towards Mount Vernon Sanctuary, or CC 12 Bartley | **Hours** Only viewable from outside | **Tip** Mount Vernon Sanctuary, a cremation cemetery on a park-like site, will only be a peaceful place for a few more years – until it becomes a new residential area.

# 64 Mustafa Centre

*The world's shop counter*

It is crowded here. Sticky. Chaotic. But there's nowhere else in Singapore like it. The department store is an institution. And if shopping is an accepted therapy, then this place can even help during the night: Mustafa is open 24 hours a day.

You can get everything here and almost everything is very cheap. Watches and jewellery, cosmetics and DVDs, blenders, suitcases, saris, spices, shoes and swimming costumes. But also massage benches, suits for children and motivational posters for your office wall. If China is the factory of the world, then Mustafa Centre is its shop counter.

Spread over almost 37,000 square metres of shopping space across four floors, it also offers a restaurant, a travel agent and a bureau de change. It was built to offer the migrant workers in Little India a piece of home, and a one-stop shopping opportunity. When you shop here you can also take out insurance, apply for a visa, book a flight home, or pick up some jewellery for your wife.

Just like the Chinese department store Tangs (see ch. 36) in the city centre, Mustafa too has a long tradition: Mustafa Ahmad, together with his son Mustaq – who still manages the shop today – and uncle Samsuddin, opened their first clothes shop in Campbell Lane in 1971. The family migrated from India in the 1950s and began with nothing at all: the father sold food from a barrow, and brought his son over later when his mother died. Mustaq only went to school for four years. But he developed a feeling for business. The Mustafa Centre opened in 1995. The concept worked: Mustaq is one of Singapore's super-rich with a fortune of more than 250 million U.S. dollars.

Electronic devices are particularly popular at Mustafa Centre, but for tourists it's the food hall that really matters: nowhere else in Singapore is there such a great selection of South Asian spices and gastronomical souvenirs.

**Address** 145 Syed Alwi Road, Singapore 207704 (Little India) | **Getting there** MRT to NE 8 Farrer Park | **Hours** Always open | **Tip** The Indian culture in Singapore is introduced interactively and with lots of loans from ethnic Indian Singaporeans in the new Indian Heritage Centre (Indianheritage.org.sg).

# 65 National Design Centre

*Gliding icons of a city*

During their training they learn how to tie their hair up in four different styles, how to apply make-up and to paint their nails red, how to glide along the aisles of an airplane and kneel down when a guest has a request. But above all they learn how to wear their *sarong kebaya* gracefully.

The robes – blue, green, red or violet depending on the rank of the wearer (while male stewards wear corresponding ties) – are iconic. Just like the 'Singapore Girls' themselves, as the Singapore Airlines flight attendants are called on the island. Even the name of the blouse-frock is international: 'sarong' comes from the Indonesian '*sarung*' and means 'covering' in Malay. *Kebaya* has its origin in the Arabic '*abaya*', for 'clothing'. The in-house tailor fits each uniform individually and always very figure-hugging; each attendant is given four per year.

'The Singapore Girl is a central brand ambassador for Singapore and a leading international brand in the travel branch,' according to the state newspaper *The Straits Times*. And it has been that way for quite a while: the elegant dress dates back to 1968. And has even made it into the National Design Centre. It was created by the French designer Pierre Balmain. Back then, today's state airline was still called Malaysia-Singapore Airlines. Balmain needed more than a year for the development – at first the stewardesses complained about the high heels of their pumps.

It wasn't until 1972 that the myth around the 'Singapore Girl' was created: the agency Batey Ads developed the campaign which still resounds today. Only the footwear had changed over the years: in a horrible plane accident the stewardesses burned their feet in their thong sandals. Since then they must wear sturdy shoes for take-off and landing. But as soon as the plane is in the air, the Singapore Girls once again glide down the aisles in their traditional sandals.

Address 111 Middle Road, Singapore 188969 | Getting there MRT to CC 2 Bras Basah |
Hours Daily 9am–9pm | Tip The Bugis Street Market is cheap for clothes and souvenirs –
Singaporeans shop here. It is usually completely crowded between the rows of small stands
(3 New Bugis Street).

# 66__ The Old Police Station
*Things weren't always so colourful here*

Yes, Singapore can be very colourful too. Opposite the leisure-heavy Clarke Quay is a grey building with rainbow-coloured window shutters. But don't think of kindergartens!

The chunky building now houses the ministry of culture, the ministry of information and some galleries. But when it was built in 1934, it was the largest police station in the city, also incorporating Singapore's first civil prison. The lettering 'Hill Street Police Station' can still be seen above the entrance. The policemen also lived in the little rooms – in those days there were 140 married and 180 single officials housed behind the shutters of the six storeys. The canteen and a hairdressing salon were on the second floor. There was even a playground on the roof for the policemen's children. Every Saturday evening, films were shown in the drill yard, which is now covered by a huge glass ceiling.

In the early years, the huge building was the biggest police headquarters on the Malaysian peninsula. The electric lifts were a special feature in those days, just like the water-flushing toilets. The large number of windows enabled good ventilation. Every officer wanted to live here and there were long waiting lists. All the same, Singaporeans were not particularly happy about the construction of the grey block with its 25,000 square metres – for them it destroyed the good feng shui of the area by the river, by obstructing the open access from Mount Faber to the water. The police moved out in 1980, and other state departments took over the house.

During Japanese occupation, the police station was used as a torture chamber. When the Allies began to bomb the city, the occupying forces painted it in brown camouflage colours – another reason that the colourful blinds of today have a liberating effect on the older generation.

And how many windows does the building have? Correct! Exactly 927.

**Address** Old Hill Street Police Station, 140 Hill Street, Singapore 179369 (Colonial District) | **Getting there** MRT to NE 5 Clarke Quay | **Hours** Galleries in the building, mostly noon–7pm | **Tip** The architecturally interesting, red and white brick building of the Central Fire Station around the corner (62 Hill Street) also contains a Civil Defence Heritage Gallery worth seeing.

# 67__The Old Train Station
*Out of time*

East Berlin immediately comes to mind, as the situation in Singapore was similar for a long time, from its separation from Malaysia in 1965 to the year 2011. In West Berlin, the S-Bahn and all its stations and lines belonged to the DDR. In Singapore, the large Tanjong Pagar Railway Station and the tracks as well as some smaller stations belonged to the neighbouring country of Malaysia. Trains from Tanjong Pagar clattered over the border towards Johor Bahru and onwards to Malacca, Kuala Lumpur and Penang.

Thankfully the monumental train station outlived the international treaties and modernisations going on all around it – it is architecturally unique. The three-storey building was built in 1932 by the Serbian architect Petrovich from the acclaimed architectural office Swan & Maclaren. A mixture of art deco, neo-classicism and local building styles, it is modelled on Eliel Saarinen's train station in Helsinki.

The initials of the Federal Malay States Railway, and four Italian statues, adorn the entrance portico under green Chinese roofs. The statues represent the cornerstones of the Malaysian economy: agriculture, trade, transport and industry. There are murals of historical Malaysian working scenes in the bright concourse, such as tin prospecting or rubber extraction.

Singaporeans love this building and its chequered history. For a whole 60 years a small but very fine hotel was housed in the station that could have competed with Raffles Hotel in service. There was a bookshop, a bureau de change, restaurants and pubs.

In 2011, thousands said goodbye to it and simultaneously greeted it – with the departure of the last train to Malaysia, the train station became Singaporean. Since then it has been kept as a national monument. No one will be able to enter it again until 2025, however, as it is being converted into part of the new Cantonment underground station. But it is worth taking a look from the outside.

Address Tanjong Pagar Railway Station, 30 Keppel Road, Singapore 089059 (Tanjong Pagar) | Getting there MRT to NE 1/CC 29 Harbour Front | Hours Only viewable from the outside for the time being | Tip The outstanding Chinese restaurant Prima Tower atop a flour mill at 201 Keppel Road is the only 360-degree revolving restaurant in the city.

# 68__ The Palace Ruins

*Light became fire*

Jungle, jungle and more jungle. In front of it a rusting gate, as tall as a man. There is nothing else to be seen of the place in which Singapore's most lavish parties were once thrown. In the corner between Tyersall Avenue and Holland Road, next to the Botanic Gardens, is a strange piece of the city. It is closed off and impenetrable. Those who have lived in Singapore for some time will still remember an exquisite forged iron gate that once blocked the way into this tropical forest.

Hidden in the forest here are the ruins of the palace of the sultan Abu Bakar. The worldly Malayan – a seasoned diplomat and friend of Queen Victoria – came from one of the families from whom the British wrangled the island of Singapore at the start of the 19th century. He became rich, not only through the appanage that the colonial rulers paid, but also through the cultivation of rubber and gambier.

The British-educated sultan certainly didn't hide his money away. He was lent an exotic note at parties in Cairo, Vienna and Budapest. When he had his palace built in Singapore on the former Tyersall Park, its inauguration was celebrated on 10 December, 1892 and de-scribed as 'Such a gathering of Singaporean society has rarely been seen' by *The Singapore Free Press*. 'The sultan was glistening in dia-monds.'

Abu Bakar certainly raised the roof: he illuminated his palace as one of the first buildings in the young city with hundreds of light bulbs. A private power plant on the site produced the electricity. But his pride and joy did not last long: in September 1905, a cable fire broke out that destroyed the palace down to its foundation walls. The sultan left it. His descendants also never returned. The green sheet metal gate to the Malaysian territory in the city state has been guarded to this day by a couple of guards in a hut. You can also find the ruins of the overgrown palace using Google Earth.

**Address** In the jungle of the square Holland Road / Tyersall Avenue, Singapore 258853 | **Getting there** Bus 7, 77, 106, 123, 174 from Orchard Boulevard to After Pierce Road, then to the left | **Hours** Palace ruins not visible, just the jungle they hide in | **Tip** You can while away a whole day in PS.Cafe over on Dempsey Hill, enjoying sumptuous Australian-style food under tropical trees.

# 69__ The Park of Evil Spirits

*Metropolitan superstition*

In Singapore everything is planned, regulated, predictable. A mini country of technocrats, a nanny state that leads its people by the hand. And yet: the unpredictable exists. There are spirits. The good ones live in the thousands of Chinese temples, in the revered trees, under some rooftops. But there are also the other ones, the evil ones. Even the government, seemingly capable of almost anything, cannot eradicate them.

And so Singaporeans believe in some bewitched patches, in hocus-pocus, in phantoms and in evil. That, for example, is supposed to rule at Bedok Reservoir. The national park was designated as 'the place of suicide' in 2011 and 2012, after the severed lower body of 23-year-old Chinese Lin Xiao, and later the body of Singaporean Tan Sze Sze and her three-year-old son were found here within a few months. Lin is thought to have been depressed, Tan was in a custody battle with her ex over their child. Five further corpse discoveries followed. Priests from the main religions held prayers by the lake at the suggestion of the former foreign minister. Perhaps equally helpful was the installation of surveillance cameras and the strengthening of police patrols.

And the most famous shopping street in Asia also has its very own dark past: in the 1950s, Orchard Road, whose shopping malls now sparkle in the centre of the city, was home to the huge Tai Shan Ting cemetery hosting almost 30,000 graves of Teochew Chinese. The underground station Dhoby Ghaut at the end of Orchard Road is in the middle of the former Jewish cemetery. The synagogue is only a stone's throw away.

You won't encounter ghosts here any more, however – you're more likely to find young people strolling in front of shop windows, loaded with shopping bags, chatting. But there are Singaporeans who would never buy an apartment here…

**Address** Bedok Reservoir Road, Singapore 479244 (Bedok), www.nparks.gov.sg/gardens-parks-and-nature | **Getting there** MRT to DT 30 Bedok Reservoir | **Hours** Always, but it is recommended to visit it in daylight, like all other parks, between 7.30am and 7.30pm | **Tip** One of Singapore's favourite specialities is Black Pepper Crab. You can unabashedly enjoy this messy food at the East Coast Seafood Centre on the coast due south of the reservoir.

# 70__Pier of the Red Lanterns

*Signals from times long gone*

Red is the colour of love. But red is also a warning light. That is no different here in Singapore than anywhere else in the world. That is why Clifford Pier is known as 'Red Lantern Harbour'. But first things first.

Today there are red lanterns set up all around the beautifully restored art deco building from the year 1933. They hardly stand out, but when the pier was still Singapore's jetty for ocean liners, a single red beacon burned on the roof. It pointed out the direction for the ships. Those who saw it knew that their destination was near.

The pier was busy in those days, it was the quay for both arrivals and departures. Thousands of immigrants passed through the vaulted foyer. The bumboats and sampans, small cargo boats, also operated here. In addition, the pier was always a stage for society: people cheered on regattas and dragon boat races here. But harrowing dramas also played out on the pier during the evacuation when the Japanese were approaching. And in the 1980s, the red lantern was given a very different meaning: the red-light district lay all around the harbour.

But things couldn't go on like this in the clean city state. Urban planners developed a new concept for the whole area: Marina Bay was created, with Clifford Pier as the jewel in the crown. The days of the immigrants, the fishermen and the prostitutes are long gone. The last bumboat departed from the pier in April 2006; the once open sea became a closed bay. But the pier radiates more beautifully than ever before – the city has invested six million Singapore dollars in its restoration. Today it belongs to the empire around the Fullerton Hotel and houses a restaurant in its tall, light-filled hall. When the pianist starts tinkling the ivories and you close your eyes tight, you can see them again: the ocean liners, which were safely guided into the harbour by the red lantern.

Address Clifford Pier, 80 Collyer Quay, Singapore 049326 (Marina Bay) | Getting there MRT to NS 26/EW 14 Raffles Place | Hours Always accessible | Tip You can enjoy the starry sky, a few drinks, and the view of Marina Bay in the Lantern Bar on the roof of the Fullerton Bay Hotel like nowhere else.

# 71_Pioneers' Memorial Hall

*Millionaires with a sense of mission*

Those who have money usually want to do something with it. If they are a generous donor or philanthropist, but quiet about it, it is up to the rest to maintain the memory of the benefactor. And so there is also a millionaires museum in Singapore.

It is hidden away in the heart of Chinatown in the Ee Hoe Hean Club, one of the city's first millionaires' clubs. Founded in 1895 and then moved into today's building in 1925, here one would interact with one's peers in a highly dignified atmosphere.

Of course, the club remains closed to guests to the city. But a door next door, with a bell that has to be rung to gain access, leads into the exquisite Pioneers' Memorial Hall. Here you can marvel at the good deeds of rich Chinese. Documents and pictures of those who came from various parts of China and made their own luck in Singapore also allow insights into the power structures of the city state.

The rich Chinese of the development years must have been a lively, politically interested bunch. They sent a lot of money to mainland China, to exert influence there and to support the development of the republic. Their figurehead, Sun Yat-sen, visited the club as well as India's prime minister Jawaharlal Nehru. In the years of the Japanese occupation during World War II, members of the club sent millions back to their old home. And thus the yellowed photos of Burma Road: reinforcements against the Japanese were supposed to roll along this road that the Americans and Burmese beat through the jungle, at great loss, towards southern China. The task of sending more than 3,000 drivers and mechanics, recruited in India and Southeast Asia, along the Burma Road, fell to the club with its China Relief Fund.

Those for whom this is all too much money and history can also have it more down to earth: around the corner from the millionaires' club is the 'association of tinned milk traders'.

Address Ee Hoe Hean Club, Level 1, 43 Bukit Pasoh Road, Singapore 089856
(Chinatown) | Getting there MRT to EW16/NE3 Outram Park | Hours Mon–Fri
9.30am–4.45pm, Sat only by appointment, guided tours at www.tkkfoundation.org.sg/
pioneers-memorial-hall | Tip Potato Head Folks on Keong Saik Road offers burgers
and cocktails on four storeys, including a rooftop garden, in a large, restored shophouse.

# 72 Plaques of the Victims

*Officer Lauterbach instigates a private war*

Today, Germans and Singaporeans work closely together. But during the two world wars, Germany and the British-administered city state were enemies. In World War I, German marines were held captive in Singapore, and during the period of Japanese occupation in World War II, German U-boat men recuperated here.

The greatest gambler of them all was the German naval officer Julius Lauterbauch. According to legend, he put the whole of Singapore in danger with a cunning trick. The survivor of the imperial warship *Emden*, which was sunk in November 1914, is said to have incited the Islamic Indian guards who held him captive. Apparently he made them believe that they would be used as cannon fodder by their British commanding officers, and would even have to fight against fellow Muslims. The Sepoy, as the Indian soldiers were called, are said to have fallen for Lauterbach's tale and the rumours spread. During the Chinese New Year celebration in the middle of February 1915, they instigated Singapore's first mutiny against the British.

The marauding soldiers shot 40 officers and civilians. But the population, including the Indians, kept their distance. The rebels were soon arrest and condemned. Eighteen of them were shot by the home guard in front of 15,000 onlookers in an ignoble public spectacle of British power. The rest were exiled to the Andaman Islands, far away from civilisation.

But the state commemorated their victims, made them into heroes. Roads were named after three of them. Plaques hanging on the left side of the main nave of the St Andrew's Cathedral commemorate the soldiers and officers who were shot. And Lauterbach? He fled in the midst of the turmoil with 34 imprisoned Germans. Travelling via Indonesia, the Philippines, China, America and Norway, he eventually made it back to Germany in October 1915, where he celebrated himself as a great adventurer.

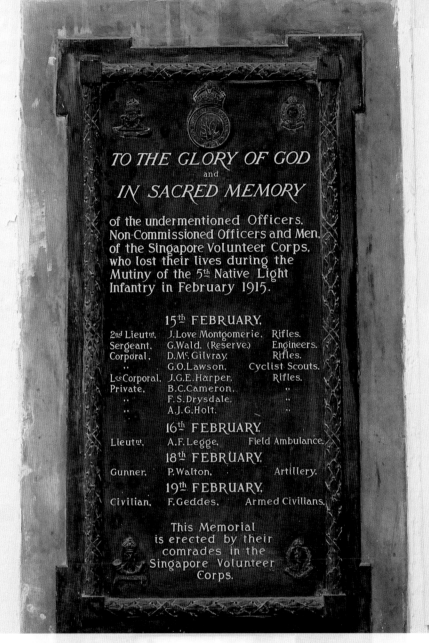

TO THE GLORY OF GOD
and
IN SACRED MEMORY

of the undermentioned Officers,
Non-Commissioned Officers and Men,
of the Singapore Volunteer Corps,
who lost their lives during the
Mutiny of the 5th Native Light
Infantry in February 1915.

### 15th FEBRUARY.

| 2nd Lieutnt. | J.Love Montgomerie. | Rifles. |
| Sergeant. | G.Wald. (Reserve.) | Engineers. |
| Corporal. | D.Mc Gilvray. | Rifles. |
| " | G.O.Lawson. | Cyclist Scouts. |
| Lce Corporal. | J.G.E.Harper. | Rifles. |
| Private. | B.C.Cameron. | " |
| " | F.S.Drysdale. | " |
| " | A.J.G.Holt. | " |

### 16th FEBRUARY.

| Lieutnt. | A.F.Legge. | Field Ambulance. |

### 18th FEBRUARY.

| Gunner. | P.Walton. | Artillery. |

### 19th FEBRUARY.

| Civilian. | F.Geddes. | Armed Civilians. |

This Memorial
is erected by their
comrades in the
Singapore Volunteer
Corps.

**Address** St Andrew's Cathedral, 11 St Andrew's Road, Singapore 178959 (Colonial District) | **Getting there** MRT to NS 25/EW 13 City Hall | **Hours** Daily 9am–5pm | **Tip** The view from the corner of Coleman Bridge and Promenade on the Singapore River guarantees a fantastic photo: the shophouses on the quay, with the skyscraper skyline in the background.

# 73 Po Chiak Keng Temple

*Where every claw counts*

The scent, the red, the gold… but the Po Chiak Keng Temple is not only sensually captivating. It is a living museum that offers us a seemingly endless series of legends and stories. Until 1982, only those with the surname Tan knew them. Only they were allowed to visit the temple, because it belonged to the Tan clan of the Chinese diaspora.

It was built more than a hundred years ago by Tan Kim Ching and Tan Beng Swee. Tan Kim Ching was the son of the philanthropist Tan Tock Seng, after whom one of the city's largest hospitals is now named. Tan Beng Swee's father donated money towards Singapore's water provision. The two sons built the Po Chiak Keng Temple, which simultaneously served as a clan house. But most important was perhaps the third function of the building: the temple was the location of a court of arbitration for the resolution of Tan family disputes. That's where the name comes from: Po Chiak Keng means the 'palace for protection of the innocent'.

There were even legal proceedings around the temple being opened up to everyone in 2007 – some Tan clan members filed a suit, but lost. Ultimately this is typical of Singapore, where religions are lived out openly and are mutually respected. Legend has it that the site was signed over to the Tans by a Chinese businessman named Tan, an Indian and a Malaysian.

The building itself is unique in Singapore. Three rooms make up the reception area. Carvings on the wooden posts and the incense pot with its dragons, that are thought to bring prosperity, are features that are found particularly in temples in southern China. If you take a closer look at the two granite dragons at the entrance, however, you may notice that they each have only three claws on their feet. This certifies that the emperor in far off Beijing had not commissioned the building of the temple – otherwise the dragons would have had five claws.

Address 15 Magazine Road, Singapore 059568 (River Valley) | Getting there MRT to NE 5 Clarke Quay | Hours Always accessible | Tip Nightlife: Zouk on Clarke Quay is a hip place to go clubbing and also organises the legendary Zouk Out Sentosa Beach Party every year.

# 74__The Presbyterian Church
*Curry with extra kick*

The small Presbyterian church sits peacefully diagonally opposite the presidential palace on Penang Road. It's hard to imagine that this Christian peace was once seriously disturbed by an atrocity. Its ingredients: an iron bar, a missing body and a huge saucepan full of curry.

Let's start from at the top of the recipe. The janitor Ayakanno Marimuthu lived behind the church with his wife and three children. In the summer of 1984 the Indian disappeared without a trace. His wife registered him as missing, but the police couldn't help. It wasn't until three years later that a police officer heard of a rumour that Marimuthu was killed in the church. So far, so bad. But after the murder, the perpetrator is said to have butchered the corpse quite professionally. Then they apparently made curry, with rice, out of the pieces in a big pot in the canteen of the church. This was then divided into portions and no, thank God, not served up, but rather packed into plastic bags and thrown into public bins.

If true, it can come as no surprise that not a single trace of the then 37-year-old janitor was ever found.

The pan and the iron bar, which was apparently used to strike the victim dead, have also never been found. But the story of the 'curry murder' was born. As in all good stories, the facts are a little blurry – for some the victim was only 34 years old, for others 38, some called him Ayakannu. But all that doesn't really matter – the horror of the curry even captivated the imagination of television producers. In 1995, the Television Corporation of Singapore dedicated an episode of its series *Doctor Justice* to the case. And the offender? They have never been convicted. Marimuthu's wife and three of her brothers were charged with murder in 1987, but there was no substantial proof and so they were all set free – the brothers only after spending four years inside.

Address 3 Orchard Road, Singapore 238825 (Centre) | Getting there MRT to NS 24/
NE 6/CC 1 Dhoby Ghaut | Hours Sun from 9am | Tip You will find very unusual Singapore
souvenirs by young local designers at Naiise in the Orchard Gateway shopping mall at
277 Orchard Road.

# 75_ The Projector
*Indie instead of Indian*

Film festivals in Singapore. The fans plod through the various auditoriums of the city. All modern, perfectly upholstered, interchange-
able places, mostly lacking charm. And then this. If you don't know
the place you'll struggle to even find the way in, straying through the
neighbouring Golden Mile Complex, beating a path between Thai
restaurants and bars, travel agents and massage salons. The complex
isn't called Little Thailand for nothing.

But it's worth taking on this adventurous trip to the cinema. And
actually it can be easy to get to: there are lifts in the entrance foyer
of the tower. Much more splendid however is the spiral staircase, an
original element in its construction in 1974.

The cinema that is so different from all the rest is on the fifth floor.
Its plain chairs give off the atmosphere of an art college cafeteria. Only
the bar is more elaborately designed. The two cinema auditoriums,
the Green Room and the Red Room, are preserved almost as they
originally were and are reminiscent of old football stadiums with
their steep rows of folding seats on concrete floors. Only the usherette
selling ice cream is missing.

The young enthusiasts who run this cinema are mainly interested
in the quality of the films shown. They want to revive the place's good
cinema tradition – at the start of the 1970s, the largest movie theatre
in the city, the 1,500-seat Golden Theatre, was located here in the
most avant-garde building of its time, with living, shopping, culture
and work in the smallest of spaces.

They have realised their dream through crowdfunding, and show
classics and the work of young filmmakers – all handpicked, indie
cinema – in the two smaller auditoriums. Money is earned on the
third floor in the main auditorium of the former Golden Theatre.
Today it is called Rex Cinema, offers almost a thousand seats and
shows Bollywood hits from India.

Address 6001 Beach Road, Suite 05-00, Golden Mile Tower, Singapore 199589 (Kampong Glam) | Getting there MRT to CC5 Nicoll Highway | Hours Tue–Fri 6.30–9pm, Sat & Sun 1–9pm | Tip The restaurant Folklore reveals a taste sensation with authentic Peranakan cuisine. In Destination hotel right next door, 700 Beach Road.

# 76 Pulau Semakau

*Phoenix from the ashes*

Admittedly, Semakau is not easy to get to. But this island off the island is something special. Here something new is growing, like a phoenix from the literal ashes. This island is made of rubbish. Or more precisely, from the ashes of rubbish. Every day, barges bring 550 tonnes of it into the huge hall on the quay of Pulau Semakau, painted bathroom green. It can be seen in the far distance from the shores of Singapore. In the hall, diggers shovel the ashes into trucks, which transport them to a dropping platform. This advances slowly, month by month, and month by month Semakau grows.

A small fishing village built on stilts once stood on the island, a good seven kilometres from the coast of Singapore. A stone's throw further on was Pulau Sakeng with a mini police station. The inhabitants were relocated in 1987 in order to make the island into a unique storage site. A seven-kilometre-long embankment has connected the islets since then, enabling them to grow together. Ashes have been deposited here since 1999. There is enough space for more ashes here until 2035.

But it would be a shame, and Singapore wouldn't be Singapore, if the new island weren't to have another purpose. Sure, there is already a small fish farm for barramundi here. But then Singapore came upon the idea to have engineers use the isolated yet so near area of land to research how green energy can be created and fed into small, independent networks. That is why Singapore's first wind turbine, an impressive 42 metres tall, is also on Semakau. Solar panels, a tidal power station and renewable materials are to follow, as well as a desalination plant. The conditions are hard – heat, moisture, tropical storms and a few rats have joined the researchers and their facilities. But ultimately they are testing the possibility of providing electricity to thousands of islands in Asia – without environmentally harmful diesel generators.

**Address** Island south-west of Singapore – can be seen from many places on the west coast, for example Labrador Park or Sentosa | **Getting there** Ferries depart from Marina South Pier, Westcoast Pier or Pasir Panjang Ferry Terminal (400 SGD); free tours are only offered by the National Environment Agency (NEA), book at least three weeks in advance at www.nea.gov.sg | **Tip** Alongside lots of space to fly kites, Marina Barrage, the Marina Bay dam, also offers a gallery exhibition about Singapore's ecological sustainability (8 Marina Gardens Drive).

# 77 — Qi Tian Gong Temple

*The monkey protects its quarter*

A building on the corner of a road junction, accessible from two sides, chairs and tables on the pavement. Such a location in Berlin or Sydney would be home to a pub. But in Singapore, the monkey king Sun Wu Kong has lived here for almost 100 years. And woe betide anyone who doubts him and his throne.

The incense sticks are smoking, the oil lamps flicker. The Qi Tian Gong Temple is dazzling with its many details and a good 10 statues of the brave and generous mythical king, who has long since become godlike. The monkey stands for power, intelligence and strength.

During the war, a Japanese bomb exploded on the road junction. The houses all around were badly damaged, and a huge crater was left gaping in the middle. Only the temple was left intact. What more evidence is needed for the strength of this god?

It is an emblem of the quarter in which it stands. Tiong Bahru is original, one of the prettiest areas of the city, as it is a late bloomer. Until the war it wasn't much more than a *kampong*, a village, with open sewers. Then came social housing and the building of the art deco flats that are so sought after today. Many flats still have their original windows and old doors. Locals christened the modern buildings '*puay kee chu*' – the 'airplane houses', as their architecture was reminiscent of airplanes or the control tower at the old Kallang Airport.

Today old and young, rich and poor, Singaporeans and immigrants live here together on the best of terms. Even the name of the quarter is made up of words from Hokkien and Malay. It means 'new graves' – before the 1920s there was a cemetery here in the mangrove forest. In the 1970s a house in Tiong Bahru cost only 18,000 SGD. Today you would pay more than a million dollars for a shoebox apartment. Good that the custodian of the monkey temple bought him his house back in 1985.

Address 44 Eng Hoon Street, Singapore 169786 (Tiong Bahru) | Getting there MRT to EW 17 Tiong Bahru | Hours Daily 7am–5pm | Tip In Singapore it is safe to say, the longer the queue, the better the food! So line up at Loo's Hainanese Curry Rice (71 Seng Poh Road).

# 78__Raffles Place MRT

*Vestiges of Singapore's oldest department store*

The heart of this financial metropolis beats at Raffles Place. Hundreds of bankers spend their lunch break in the shadows of the financial institutions' skyscrapers around the bright green square. But there is a lot going on underground here too. Two white entrances to the subterranean MRT, built in a Neoclassicist colonial style, stand opposite one another and mark the ends of the square. They are the most striking of the 10 entrances and seem to come from a completely different time, reminders of the mid-19th century, when this place still looked like a grand square in London. Majestic colonial buildings lined the open space where people wanted to see and be seen, strolling around and shopping, just like on the Orchard Road of today.

The two gable ends of the entrances show the aspect of the former John Little Department Store. For decades it held the status of the oldest department store in Singapore and was the favoured place for European delegates to shop. In 1842, John Little, of Irish descent, opened his store on Raffles Place, which was still called Commercial Square at the time. After a partnership with a Parsi businessman, he then ran the store with his brother under the name John Little & Co. The company became very successful in the wine and spirits market, traded in books, sold clocks and even conducted business in neighbouring Malaya.

But in 1955, John Little was taken over by Robinsons, the second-biggest store on the square. The John Little name lived on, but the offering was only made up of Robinsons' cheaper segments. In 1960, after 118 years, John Little moved from the square to Orchard Road and opened several branches. But not even the new brand name, JL, could save it: the traditional department store closed the doors of its last shop in Plaza Singapura in 2017. All that remains are memories. And the two reliefs on the little buildings that lead to the underground.

Address Raffles Place, Singapore 048616 (Central Business District) | Getting there MRT to EW14/NS26 Raffles Place | Hours Always accessible | Tip 1-Altitude in the One Raffles Place skyscraper is the highest roof-bar in Singapore. The 360-degree view is fantastic, but short trousers are a no-go!

# 79__ The Raffles Statues
## *The black man and the white man*

Was Singapore's British founder Sir Stamford Bingley Raffles in fact black? Most certainly not. And yet the Malays who witnessed the unveiling of the first statue of the city's founder at the end of June 1887 believed precisely this. 'He was one of us,' they are said to have called out in astonishment. But quite understandably: the statue of the East India Company delegate was jet black.

A second – white – Raffles stands only a stone's throw away on the British landing site on the Singapore River. He is, so to speak, the official Raffles. The smaller black figure was first moved to its current location in front of the Victoria Theatre and Concert Hall in 1919. Black and white were to play yet another role here: it was at this spot precisely that Singaporeans were given the chance to watch the first black-and-white broadcast from their new television station on 17 televisions in 1963. The film TV *Looks at Singapore* was 15 minutes long and a good 500 people are thought to have been at the premiere.

The black Raffles is very lucky still to be around. In 1942, the Japanese occupiers of the city were planning to melt him down. It is only due to the brave Japanese director of the national museum that he survived the occupation. He reported to Tokyo that the statue was destroyed, when in reality he had it stored in the cellar of the museum. And so the black Raffles could be reinstalled in 1946.

But shortly afterwards, even Singapore's perpetual ruling party wanted to get rid of the founder of their city. At the climax of the anti-colonial movement, the People's Action Party planned to eradicate the memory of the colonial rulers. Thankfully, the more rational politicians in the party decided against denying their own history. Both black and white could once again breathe easy. After around 200 exciting years, they are currently enjoying a peaceful coexistence.

Address Raffles Landing Site on the quay in front of Old Parliament House, 1 Old Parliament Lane, and in front of Victoria Theatre & Concert Hall, 9 Empress Place, Singapore (Colonial District) | Getting there MRT to NS 26/EW 14 Raffles Place | Tip On the quay you can board one of the picturesque bumboats decorated with red lanterns and take a cruise of Marina Bay. It is particularly romantic at night.

# 80_ The Red House
*Tinder from 1925*

It should smell of coffee and cake here, but it doesn't. At least, not like it used to. Despite everyone trying hard to revive the good old days. But those days are so far in the Red House Bakery's past that it isn't easy.

The Katong Bakery & Confectionery opened here in the 1920s. The Red Bakery, as it was soon called because of the colour of its facade, was a favourite place for neighbours for breakfast. But the café had the feel of a Viennese coffeehouse, with the old owners serving their guests, who sat at marble tables and on Bauhaus chairs. The bakery was founded by a Jewish man called Jim Baker, a Chinese man took it over in 1931. The building, however, belonged to an Islamic foundation, or Wakaf, having been bequeathed by the great-granddaughter of Hajjah Fatimah (see ch. 10). It was well known for its curry puffs and Swiss rolls, but also for its matchmaking: in the times before Tinder, parents brought their offspring together here behind folding screens, so that they could fall in love with each other in peace over a slice of cake.

But in 2003 the Red House was deemed structurally unsafe. It was closed, and all the furnishings, right down to the boards on which the cakes cooled, went to museums and collectors. The people who had run it moved into a nursing home, and for a long time the building disappeared behind a tall site fence. But years later the Red Bakery has finally been reborn, restored, refreshed. The establishment has been restored with great effort, old building components have been used, even the firing of the floor tiles in the old style is a story in itself. To reproduce the old windows, the only Singaporean craftsman who was still capable of the job had to be called out of retirement.

Now it is run by the local coffeehouse chain, Wang Café, and for matchmaking you simply swipe to the right on Tinder.

Address 63 East Coast Road, Singapore 428782 (Katong) | Getting there MRT to CC 8 Dakota, then bus 10 to Opposite Roxy Square | Hours Daily 7.30am – 9.30pm | Tip There are rows of splendid shophouses on Koon Seng Road. Pastel colours, decorated with stucco and bat emblems, they are a West-East mixture of styles.

# 81 Roast Paradise

*To paradise via pork belly*

The Roast Paradise shop front measures less than two metres. Behind the window hang pork bellies, shiny with fat and marinade. On the glass itself are newspaper clippings that sing the praises of the *char siew* (barbecue) that is served here. And there are always at least 10 people queuing up in front of the stall from 11.30am, wanting to indulge themselves for 3.80 Singapore dollars.

The food at Roast Paradise is delicious. The hawkers, as the fast-food stands at the food markets in Singapore are called, are typical for the city. Food brings people together, and the way to friendship here is through the stomach. Or, as Singapore's friendliest poster boy, the ambassador-at-large Tommy Koh, says: 'One of the glues that sticks us together as a young country with various ethnicities and religions is our street food.'

Its face could be Yu Zhen Kai. The young man first grafted away at Kentucky Fried Chicken, then he entertained seriously rich men with loose women. But ultimately he learned a real trade from his uncle in Malaysia: to roast pork belly like no one else, at 400 degrees, over three hours, in an oven from China, and then to dip it in a marinade that is made of 18 ingredients and whose outstanding recipe he will one day take with him to the grave.

This makes Yu quite typical of the city's numerous hawkers. So far four assistants work for him in his six-square-metre mini-kitchen, all of them former prisoners. The rent costs him around 3,000 Singapore dollars a month, but the hawkers in the city state don't have to pay taxes – their art is seen, so to speak, as a cultural asset of Singapore and eligible for support. And because the demand for his speciality – like most hawkers, Yu only serves one dish – is so big, he can survive. But he still has to work from six in the morning to ten in the evening, while dreaming of one day building up a culinary empire.

烧味天堂

ROAST PARADISE *Since 1970.*

#soshiokpork

01-121

Sinful char siew

**Address** 51 Old Airport Road, Suite 01-121 Old Airport Road Food Centre, Singapore 390051 (Katong) | **Getting there** MRT to CC 8 Dakota | **Hours** Tue–Sun 11am–7pm | **Tip** Artists, courses, exhibitions – the Goodman Arts Centre (90 Goodman Road) offers all that as well as an Italian restaurant and an artists café (www.goodmanartscentre.sg).

# 82_ The Sand Reserve
*Built on sand*

In Singapore the beach is precisely where it should be – by the sea. But Singapore's only dunes are right in the middle of the city. Huge mountains of sand rise up near Bedok Reservoir (sometimes called 'the place for suicides', see ch. 69). Running up them or rolling down them is, however, strictly prohibited. A double green fence and lots of cameras prevent dune climbers. But there is good reason for this: the sand is Singapore's future.

A sign at the entrance to the site confirms this, stating that these are the reserves of the HDB. The abbreviation stands for Housing Development Board, but is used colloquially for social housing. Eighty-five per cent of citizens own one of these apartments, which the government has heavily subsidised. In order to be able to continue building them, Singapore needs sand. But in the meantime this has became a scarce resource in Asia due to the construction boom. The price for sand has shot through the roof, and in Myanmar, Cambodia, Vietnam or Indonesia, sand merchants illegally dig up beaches and river beds to meet demand. The governments do try to prevent this, but deliveries to Singapore have already suffered from strikes.

The government has learned from this and has set up a sand reserve. After all, the state wants to grow. Since its foundation, it has grown around a quarter in size due to land reclamation – sand is needed for that too. Practically the whole of Singapore's financial district beyond Beach Road is built on reclaimed land – the banks of the financial metropolis are built on literal rather than proverbial sand.

Independent of the strategic sand reserve in Bedok, Singapore increasingly uses the excavated material from the tunnelling for the rapidly growing underground network, to reclaim land off the coast. The gold that Singapore mines is sometimes nothing more than plain old earth.

Address Tampines Avenue 10 by Bedok Reservoir, Singapore 529771 (Bedok) | Getting there MRT to EW5 Bedok, then bus 137 to Before Barclay Viaduct | Hours Only viewable from the outside | Tip Satisfy your spirit of adventure at the climbing park Forest Adventure at Bedok Reservoir, offering a climbing course in the trees and a zip wire over the lake.

# 83__ The School Mural

*Ice Ball and Army Market*

The painted walls of the former Sino-English Catholic School are like windows into a past life, presenting scenes from Singapore between the 1930s and the 1960s. In the summer of 2016 a state secretary even came to inaugurate them – the city and the government endeavour to preserve the traditions. They want to create a sense of community among Singaporeans.

The colour pictures show the loaning out of books in the long since demolished Old National Library, but even today still has a great collective memory value. The old Odeon cinema, in which generations of Singaporeans learned to kiss, the mum & pop shop around the corner, an army market, where you could buy the gear for military service, and an ice ball – the shaved ice flavoured with syrups, red-bean paste, evaporated milk, grass jelly and palm fruit that traders sold in front of schools from their bicycle rickshaws in the 1960s.

Most interesting though is the picture of the Two Rails: here we can see the tracks of the railroad coming from Malaysia, and next to it a portrait of Father Edward Becheras. The French missionary founded the school that was located here for decades in 1935. The bearded man spoke about the path of his school being double tracked: the children were to be educated equally in English and Mandarin – like today's bilingual education.

The Sino-English Catholic School moved to Bishan in 1992, and lists the Prime Minister Lee Hsien Loong among its former pupils. But until that move, it lived in this building on the grounds of the Church of Saints Peter and Paul, a centre for the city's Chinese Catholics. The French influence of the missionary can be felt here too: the colourful glass windows and the bells were brought to Singapore from France. And Father Becheras' pupils used the churchyard for their sports lessons.

# 84__The Scottish Market Hall
*Old love never rusts*

Where is the centre of Singapore? Where does its heart beat? In Fort Canning, where the city's founder Raffles resided? Around the parliament? At the Istana, the governmental palace? All wrong. It is Lau Pa Sat, the old market. Singapore has had changes of ruler and governmental forms, but has always been a trading place. And nowhere else can match the tropical island in this – everything that isn't screwed down is traded here, from financial derivatives to fish, from wheat to weapons. That's why the market in the heart of the city is its true centre.

The market was first built in the Chinese quarter in 1823: the Telok Ayer Market must have been a rather rickety wooden construction on Market Street, with stilts lifting it out of Telok Ayer Bay. When land was reclaimed for the growth of the city in 1879, it moved towards Collyer Quay and became two-storey. In 1894, the engineer James MacRitchie – after whom one of the reservoirs is named – then built a construction out of steel arches forged in Scotland. An open, airy, octagonal hall, was created. It was only in 1989 that the market was renamed Lau Pa Sat, which is Hokkien and means precisely what the building is: 'old market'.

Since 1973 the market has been a food court in the middle of Singapore's continually growing financial district. However, it was forced to shut down while an underground line was being built. As Singapore, thank goodness, already recognised the value of the old iron construction at the time, the girders were mothballed for a few years. Long been considered an icon of the colonial period, the renovated market with its real old girders and ornate supporting arches from Glasgow is now cared for and protected. Since its ventilation was improved, business has also picked up again. Up to 20,000 guests sit under the Scottish iron construction every day enjoying tropical hawker cuisine.

Address Lau Pa Sat, 18 Raffles Quay, Singapore 048582 (Central Business District) |
Getting there MRT to NS 26/EW 14 Raffles Place, DT 17 Downtown | Hours Always
open | Tip Had enough fried food? You can put together your own well-balanced and
delicious 'green' food meal at Grain Traders at 138 Market Street.

# 85 __ SG50 Markers

*Gilded path from yesterday into tomorrow*

Best foot forward! That's the basic message of the plaques set into the ground in the inner city. They mark the young republic's most important day of celebration thus far: on 9 August, 2015, the city state celebrated the 50th anniversary of its foundation. The abbreviated form is SG50 – which can now be read on the round bronze plaques here and there throughout the city, together with the lettering 'Singapore's Golden Jubilee'.

An estimated two million people took part in the jubilee celebrations. These ranged from the best jubilee dessert to the biggest fireworks, from an additional holiday and specially printed bank notes to a goodie bag for each household containing erasers decorated with the country's flag. A city map of hearts was created from the contributions of 80,000 participants who revealed their favourite places in Singapore: the 50 most frequently mentioned places, among them Changi Airport, were marked with a red heart as 'home places'.

But the jubilee was much more than an oversized ceremony: politicians used it to give the young state a feeling of nationality. The fathers of the city had an eight-kilometre-long Jubilee Walk marked out, leading to 25 – mostly historic – sights. It begins at the National Museum and runs from the colonial building to the dam of Marine Barrage at the end of Gardens by the Bay. Not everywhere, but particularly along Marina Bay, the plaques in the ground point the way. They are similar to the golden *Stolpersteinen* by the artist Gunter Demnig, that commemorate the extermination of the Jews in many German cities – only that the golden plaques in Singapore give reason to celebrate. Even though the colonial buildings on the Jubilee walk are also acclaimed, it is quite rightly the pride in what Singapore has made of itself since its independence in 1965 that dominates.

**Address** All over the colonial district, most near the Esplanade, Singapore 038981 | **Getting there** MRT to CC 3 to Esplanade | **Tip** At the weekend there are free performances by local bands, classical orchestras or theatre groups in the Outdoor Theatre river side of the Esplanade (1 Esplanade Drive).

# 86 __ Sky Garages
*A parking space in your living room*

There are people who like their cars. There are people who love them. And there are people who love them so much that they don't even want to be separated from them at night. They park within sight, and now and then they gaze from the living room window at their sports car. In Singapore, you can go a step further, and do this even if you live in a high rise.

KOP Properties has created the first apartment high rise in Asia in which the super rich can park their cars at dizzying heights. Two glass elevators in the Multiparker 720 system built by the Swabian manufacturer Wöhr lift them at 2.8 metres a second up to the parking space that belongs to each apartment. There, only a pane of glass separates the living room from the double garage. So while watching a Formula 1 race on the television, the wealthy can always cast a glance across to their own sports cars.

The building is right in the centre of Singapore. And so others let their gazes wander too: the architects from AMA Architects modified the former hotel so that the two glass automobile elevators are at the left and right front corners of the high rise. At night they are illuminated in all the colours of the rainbow. When a Maserati speeds towards the sky, the hardened Singaporean taxi drivers watch too. They know the real price of what is being lifted here: the two lifts move around quarter of a million euros up and down every day.

Once they arrive at their destination, the owners are no longer able, due to safety reasons, to touch their cars on the other side of the huge glass wall – the orange Lamborghinis are like sleeping lizards in a terrarium. Unloading the shopping? No longer possible. Giving the car a wash? Certainly not. But still the luxury apartments come at a price: the 250-square-metre apartments cost upwards of 10 million Singapore dollars since the conversion in 2010.

Address Hamilton Scotts, 37 Scotts Road, Singapore 228229 (Centre) | Getting there MRT to NS 21/DT 11 Newton | Tip Spotless business idea: Holistic Sneaker Laundry on Wheelock Place (501 Orchard Road) washes designer sneakers. There would seem to be a demand.

# 87___The Soya Sauce Factory
*Years of maturation*

Master Woo and his extended family tend to a delicious inheritance: soya sauce. Very few still produce it in the traditional way in Singapore as it is very work and time intensive. That doesn't dissuade the manufacturer – even in times of profit maximisation, Woo is only guided by the very high quality of his products. And he wants to continue the family tradition.

Only those in the know find their way to the factory as it is in one of Singapore's many small industrial estates. But it is worth the visit as one of the best soya sauces in the world is produced by hand and sold here.

Seventy-four years ago the grandfather brought the recipe from China to Singapore. The sauces continue to be made exactly as they were back then: the beans are steamed and rolled in a mixture of flour and a fermentation fungus. This is hard physical work; the men are often up to their elbows in the beans. Later they put them into barrels and douse them in brine. Then the tropical sun does its work: the barrels are sealed and left in the heat to ferment.

The longer, the better, as it is this step that gives the sauce its complex flavour, just like a good wine or cheese. The Woo family's light soya sauce matures for a year, the dark version for one and a half years. The factory yard is therefore full of maturing barrels; its sheer floor space is the measure of how many litres are currently being manufactured.

The cheap sauces are now fermented in two days. Two days compared to one and a half years – that makes the difference. Woo's customers venerate every drop of his sauce: it has certainly found its admirers and can therefore survive in its connoisseur niche. But the Woo family recognise the signs of the times too: the young, educated Woo has diversified the range and extended it to include other products. This way the delicious inheritance can survive for the next generation.

Address Kwong Woh Hing Sauce Factory, 5 Defu Lane 9, Singapore 539247 (Paya Lebar) |
Getting there MRT to CC 12 Bartley, then by taxi | Hours Mon–Fri 8am–5pm, Sat
8am–3pm | Tip The Singaporean air defence system is interactively represented in the Air
Force Museum at 400 Airport Road.

# 88 The Solar Raft in Tuas
*Sun on the water*

Singapore sits one degree north of the equator. The sun shines here. And energy is used here – for light and washing machines, but especially for air-conditioning. So nothing comes more natural than tapping the sun's power. And of course here too Singapore attempts to be at the forefront. The National University's solar institute, SERIS, is therefore carrying out tests on solar rafts on the water – after all, anyone can do roofs, and the tropical island doesn't have large unused areas of land like India or Australia for example, with their huge solar farms.

The idea of the floating solar factory is promising: if researchers in the city state manage to build working rafts with solar panels, a portion of the reservoirs could be covered with them. This would bring with it several advantages: there are many hectares of surface space available, and the temperature of the upper layer of water would be reduced and thus less water would evaporate. The researchers also hope that the lower temperatures under the solar panels would slow down the rapid growth of algae in the waters under the tropical sun.

To begin with, the scientists are trying out the materials on a small raft directly opposite the border-crossing to Malaysia in Tuas. The shore is hard to access, a golf club and a police training ground are nearby. The panels are optimally oriented towards the tropical sun and the electricity produced is already being used. If the trials work, then there will very soon be solar rafts like these anchored on many of Singapore's reservoirs. The scientists can imagine that a fifth of the water surface could be covered.

But the generation of energy on the surface of the water will only really start to become attractive when similar devices can be successfully deployed on the sea. Singapore wants to test this out too, probably off the artificially reclaimed island of Semakau.

Address Tengeh Reservoir, Singapore 638410 (Tuas) | Getting there MRT to EW 33 Tuas Link, then taxi, on Jalan Ahmad Ibrahim take the last U-turn before the border in the direction of the city and turn off onto the first small road to the left | Hours Can only be viewed from a distance, except for specialists | Tip It's worth paying a visit to the restaurant at the nearby Raffles Marina, where you can sit and enjoy the sunset over the masts of the boats and the lighthouse.

# 89_ The Southernmost Point
*On the island off the island off the island*

At the end there is nothing but water. And then the Indonesian Sumatra, directly opposite. A couple of container ships in between, on the way from China to Rotterdam or Hamburg. Let's be honest: there isn't really anything much to see here on this rock. But still the island off the island off the island is a very special place for Singapore. As here, according to the city's fathers, with the energetic support of the tourist office, is the southernmost point of continental Asia.

Continental Asia? By this they mean the Eurasian landmass that stretches uninterrupted from Portugal in the west to the tropical state on the equator. They have built three bridges in order to stretch it a little further to the south – the first goes from Malaysian Johor Bahru to Singapore, the second onto its pleasure island Sentosa. From here, on Palawan Beach, a narrow suspension bridge hangs over the water to get onto the rock that is identified as the southernmost part of the continent. Here a plain wooden sign awaits superlative-seeking visitors with the information that they have finally reached their destination: 'The Southernmost Point of Continental Asia'. A second sign with a map declares that the equator is another 136 kilometres from here.

Two wooden lookout towers have been built so that the rock experience isn't all too barren – painted dark brown, with pagoda roofs and connected to one another by a walkway. On a good day the view from up here almost stretches all the way to the new industrial zone of Tuas in western Singapore.

And that's the problem: the southernmost point has never been here. Tanjong Beach a couple of hundred metres away is further south, and Singapore's land reclamation has ensured that Tuas, wrested from the sea, is also a good bit closer to the equator. But tourists never go there. And you certainly won't find any signs making the claim there either.

Address Palawan Beach, Singapore 099981 (Sentosa) | Getting there MRT to NE 1/ CC 29 HarbourFront, then Sentosa Express to Beach Station | Hours Always accessible | Tip The Tanjong Beach Club at Tanjong Beach provides loungers, drinks and music, so you can just chill.

# 90　Speakers' Corner
*Talking, if the police allow*

Amos Yee has a sad sort of celebrity in Singapore. For some the young Singaporean, who was granted political asylum in America at the end of March 2017, is an icon of freedom of speech. For others he is someone who spreads hate and trouble. The blogger had voiced insulting opinions about Singapore's founding father Lee Kuan Yew and some religions. But the American judge declared that Singapore 'persecuted Yee because of his political opinions'.

Freedom of opinion and speech isn't an easy topic in Singapore. The constitution of the city state does ensure these rights, but the government has the power to restrict them. And it does. Lawsuits are filed against critics time and again – and this even though the highly respected former ambassador Tommy Koh, for example, calls on the city state to respect 'challengers, who are subversive and have alternative points of view'.

Singapore likes to point to Speakers' Corner in Hong Lim Park when it is criticised. A wooden sign above a park bench marks the corner on the edge of the financial district. Here you can say what you wish – as long as you register your speech with the police beforehand. But that too isn't simple, for example, when an- nually draws attention to its concerns there on Pink Dot day. In other places in the world there are large gay pride parades, and just like there, an increasing number of companies support the LGBT community in their year event at Speakers' Corner in Singapore. But in the summer of 2016 the interior minister demanded that foreigners should not become involved. This order affects global companies such as Goldman Sachs, Apple, Facebook, Microsoft or Visa. 'Under the rules that apply for Speakers' Corner for events such as Pink Dot, foreigners are not allowed to organise anything, or to speak or to take part in the demonstrations,' the ministry de- clared. Full stop.

Address 20 Upper Pickering Street, Singapore 058284 (Chinatown) | Getting there MRT to NE 4/DT 19 Chinatown | Tip The Parkroyal hotel on Pickering opposite, with its organic forms, green terraces and facades and over-sized Chinese bird cages, is an architectural icon.

# 91 St Andrew's Cathedral

*Coconut bricklayers*

The inside of the coconut is edible. You can grate it into soup, or coat it in chocolate and turn it into bars. Indians smash the nut against the ground in front of their temples so that the white flesh of the fruit testifies to their purity. But bricklayers also like the nut. At least they liked it in previous centuries when they came from India.

St Andrew's Cathedral gleams with snow-white walls. The foundation stone of the oldest Anglican house of worship in Singapore was laid in 1856. But the first church burned down after being hit twice by lightning.

Its successor was constructed by Indian convicts, who had been shipped to the new British colony in the tropics for this very purpose. For the plaster they used a mixture of shell limestone, egg white, coarse sugar (jaggery), water and sometimes lemon juice, into which they stirred coconut flesh. After it had hardened, the walls were then polished with hard stones and finally sprinkled with a powder made of soapstone, which not only lent the walls a soft surface, but also made them gleam. This *madras chunam*, as the plaster is called, was also used by the Tamil master builders on Serangoon Road to create ornaments on the houses there.

The first group of convicts came from south India to Singapore in 1825. Some of the forced labourers were allowed to stay after working off their punishment, others were later relocated to the Andaman Islands. They were instructed in their work on many of the prestigious buildings by the British major and engineer John Frederick Adolphus McNair. He saw more in them than just slave labourers: McNair had learned photography in 1861, and when he returned to Singapore, he took photos of 'his' prisoners. Then he taught them photography too. It wasn't long until this became a tourist attraction, as people deliberately came to the prison to have their photographs taken by McNair's convicts.

**Address** 11 St Andrew's Road, Singapore 178959 (Colonial District) | Getting there MRT to NS 25/EW 13 City Hall | **Hours** Daily 9am–5pm | Tip Opposite is Capitol Singapore with three listed buildings, many shops, restaurants and soon a luxury hotel.

# 92 __ St George's Glass Windows

*The chaplain takes his secret to his grave*

The church stands solemn and silent on the edge of the loud party district of Dempsey Hill. The red-brick building is built like a hall with a saddle roof and no tower. In this way the former garrison church fitted in with the architecture of the military barracks that surrounded it at the time.

However, the small house of worship stands out nonetheless thanks to its facade. The orange-red bricks from India were laid artistically with decorative ornamentation and openings for ventilation. The British architect William H. Stanbury designed the church in 1910 in the classical Romanesque style. The large window openings are furnished with round arches. On one side they are filled with white wooden slats, on the other side with colourful glass windows.

These hide the secret of the church – they were only installed in 1955. There are a number of legends surrounding the originals. When Singapore was fighting in World War II against the advancing Japanese, the British troops were located in Dempsey Hill. St George's was their garrison church and was furnished with valuable stained-glass windows. The then British chaplain wanted to save them from destruction and therefore buried them in a secret place that only he knew. After the Japanese victory, the clergyman became a prisoner of war and died, like thousands of others, in one of the camps in Singapore.

After the war an intensive search for the windows began. Without success. Then a soldier from the British camp in Changi claimed that they had been buried there shortly before the fall of the city, but this excavation was as fruitless as all the others that followed over the decades. This has nurtured the rumour that the missing windows were destroyed in an air raid on the harbour before their voyage to safety in Australia. The chaplain never had the chance to disclose his secret.

Address 44 Minden Road, Singapore 248816 (Tanglin) | Getting there Bus 7, 77, 106, 123, 174 from Orchard Boulevard to Opposite Botanic Gardens | Hours Mon – Sat 8.30am – 4.30pm, Sun 8am – 6.30pm | Tip The former Ebenezer chapel, a little further along the road, now houses the restaurant The White Rabbit in its large nave.

# 93 The Stone Steps
*When bricks talk*

Arrows can kill. Or specify a direction. But in Singapore's old Botanic Gardens they tell a story – a story of suffering and hope, of pride and resistance.

After 1942, Singapore's Japanese occupiers forced Australian prisoners of war in the Changi camp to fire bricks. The Australian troops had helped to defend the city, under British leadership, against the assault of the Japanese. After they had been overwhelmed and Singapore capitulated there were terrible scenes. The treatment of prisoners of war in the camps was also inhumane. Hunger, thirst and torture were part of the daily routine. But the Australians at the brick ovens did something to counter this: they marked their stones. They scratched an arrow in each of them before they were baked. Sometimes crooked, sometimes skewed, sometimes large, sometimes small, sometimes even pointing in both directions. But the arrows were always clearly recognisable. Why? In the colonial days, the property of the government was often marked with arrows. In this way the prisoners 'pointed' out that they were currently the property of the Japanese administration.

From 20 February, 1942 the Botanic Gardens were run by the Japanese geologist Hidezo Tanakadate. He had stairs built from today's Lower Ring Road to the Plant House. He used the Australian prisoners to carry out the work. The guards didn't realise that most of the stones were marked. Or at least they didn't understand the message.

The silent protest first became known a good half-century later: in 1995 eight former Australian prisoners of war visited Singapore, the place of their enslavement and torture. They absolutely insisted on seeing the small flight of stairs in the Botanic Gardens. When they were taken there, smiles broke out across the faces of the old men. And they began to tell the story…

Address Botanic Gardens, 1 Cluny Road, Singapore 259569 (Tanglin) | Getting there MRT to CC 19/DT 9 Botanic Gardens, bus 7, 77, 106, 123, 174 from Orchard Boulevard to Opposite Botanic Gardens | Hours Daily 5am–midnight | Tip If you're feeling a strange longing for German food, you'll find it in Huber's Butchery restaurant and shop at 22 Dempsey Road, opposite the gardens.

# 94 The Strait of Malacca

*Deliver oil, buy televisions*

When you hear the word 'strait', you may think of a narrow and rather unimportant stretch of water. But the Strait of Malacca is more like a superhighway of the high seas and its importance is more than evident.

The lower end of the strait begins directly off the coast of Singapore, one degree and 15 minutes north of the equator. The lifeline between the east and west, between the South China Sea and the Andaman Sea, measures 800 kilometres. It is the shortest water route from the sales market of Europe and the oil states of Arabia to East Asia and the factories of the world, to China, Korea and Japan. Tanker upon tanker laden with liquid gas and oil crawl in one direction, container ships with televisions, clothes, furniture in the other. Those who live on Sentosa, the island of Singapore's multimillionaires, can survey the condition of world trade in its daily rhythm from their balconies via binoculars.

The number of ships sailing along the Silk Road of the sea increases continually. In the year 2000 the number was still at 64,000 ships. In 2015 it was 222 ships a day, an average of 5 more than in 2014 – with 81,000 ships for the year, a record for the strait. On the axis of globalisation, more oil is transported in one day than is used in a week across the whole of Germany.

The Strait of Malacca really brings the effects of globalisation into focus. The division between rich and poor, between winners and losers, is rarely as evident as along its shores: on this side is ultra-rich Singapore, with its luxury yachts and villas, on the other side the coast of Sumatra with its huts and villages in the mist. Of course there are also pirates here: they regularly attack the mid-size cargo ships in particular, to steal money and copper and brass parts. Sometimes they even hijack a ship to extort a ransom or pump out all of the oil from tankers.

Address Sentosa Cove on Ocean Drive on Sentosa | Getting there MRT to CC 29/ NE 1/S HarbourFront, then take the white Sentosa Cove Shuttle Bus | Tip At Greenwood Fish Market on Quayside Isle (31 Ocean Way) there is fresh fish and seafood as well as a marvellous view of the harbour.

# 95 __ The Substation

*Highly charged location*

The Substation doesn't exactly have a modest location. It sits right in the heart of historic Singapore, with the Peranakan Museum to the left, the National Museum to the right, and behind it Fort Canning, where the story of the city began. And yet the former electricity substation fits in well here. The Singapore Management University with its thousands of students and the LASALLE College of the Arts are also only a stone's throw away. Just like them, the structure from the 1920s embodies, with its four grey columns and windows of green glass, a new Singapore. A different one.

Up until the 1970s, the power plant was still producing power, with workers storing machinery and cable drums in its garden. Then the bulky structure was left vacant. But since the 1990s it has once again been a highly charged location. The dramatist Kuo Pao Kun had suggested transforming the decaying building into a centre for visual art. At the same time, a preservation order was put on several neighbouring buildings along Armenian Street. One million Singapore dollars and four years later, in 1990, the new Substation opened its doors.

It was like an act of liberation: suddenly the metropolis' long-overlooked art scene had a home. And what a home it is. Kuo was its founder and first artistic director. He opened his building to groups who now lead the way in the city's art scene, but who at the time were not well known at all. Here, even before the turn of the millennium, they could experiment, take chances, almost as if there was neither censorship nor guardians of public morals in Singapore. Literature, dance, theatre and music suddenly had a kind of protected space – of course only within the state's limits, which were, thankfully, interpreted broadly here. The programme has been underpinned since 1993 by art conferences that dare to question what counts as dominant opinion in the city.

Address 45 Armenian Street, Singapore 179936 (Colonial District) | Getting there
MRT to CC 2 Bras Basah | Hours Mon – Fri 10am – 7pm, except during events | Tip You
will find contemporary art in the Mulan Gallery, a little way further along the street.

# 96__ The Swiss Club

*Beautiful swimming at the state's expense*

The Swiss understandably don't like to hear it, but their clubhouse is somehow reminiscent of a dwarf's house. Red window shutters, little towers, old trees all around. Nonetheless, millions have changed hands here over the years. The club itself, since its merger with the German Club, is wealthy. And its members, who work for Roche, DKSH, UBS, Nestlé and the like, all have money too.

But things didn't always run so smoothly for the Swiss in Singapore. They built their first clubhouse – a wooden hut with an accompanying shooting range – on land that belonged to the Chinese trading company Whampoa. They soon had to move. Almost 30 Swiss then bought a site from French missionaries for 3,750 Straits dollars and extra land for a pool on the Bukit Tinggi hill. At the opening in 1902 there was a six-course-meal and the 3rd Madras Light Infantry Band played. But the building burned down in 1909. The circumstances around its destruction were never clarified, but Syed Abdul Kader Alsagoff, sheik and co-owner of the Raffles Hotel, had been shot beforehand – with Swiss ammunition from a Swiss pistol. Suspicion fell on a Malaysian guard from the club, who was then fired. Did he take revenge?

The third attempt was a beautiful wooden house, replaced in 1927 by this fairy-tale building by the Swiss architect Heinrich Rudolf Arbenz. It was extremely modern, with electric lights and changing cubicles. But the Swiss wouldn't have been truly Swiss if they hadn't saved on expenses where possible, having their huge pool financed by the British municipal administration by convincing them that it served to dry out the area that was infested by malaria mosquitoes.

The building is no longer the main focus of the grounds, surrounded now by a Swiss school, pool, tennis courts and a modern guesthouse. But it is comfortable nonetheless, and they serve rösti too.

Address 36 Swiss Club Road, Singapore 288139 (Bukit Timah) | Getting there MRT to DT 17 Sixth Avenue, then by taxi | Hours Inquiries at www.swissclub.org.sg | Tip Violet Kwan is the Grande Dame of cake bakers. You will find delicious cakes made to old family recipes at her Lana Cake Shop (36 Greenwood Avenue).

# 97__Tan Tock Seng's Grave
*Singapore's big patron*

If you want to track down this grave you really have to do some searching. It is supposed to be on the edge of the hip area of Tiong Bahru, but even many locals don't know it. You will find it completely hidden on the slope near Pearl's Hill, almost overgrown with greenery. A simple, typical Chinese stone grave, the only decorations on it are the small, sculpted lions. A place of peace, even though the hill is bordered by the multi-lane Outram Road and Eu Tong Sen Street.

Everything began on Pearl Hill – this is where Tan Tock Seng had his first paupers' hospital built in 1844. Under British colonial rule, the medical care of the poor was so inadequate that many had to live in the streets of the city. Tan wanted to change this. The Hokkien Chinese businessman, who had become very wealthy, donated $5,000 for its construction, a princely sum at that time.

Himself an immigrant from a poor background in Malacca, he first earned his money in the emerging colonial city of Singapore as a fruit and poultry seller. He worked hard and built up a business on Boat Quay, but it was his business relations with an English merchant, connected with successful real estate deals, that made him one of the most wealthy citizens of the city.

Highly respected by the Chinese population, they called him the 'captain of the Chinese'. But he also enjoyed huge respect among the colonial rulers – they appointed him the first Chinese man to take the role of justice of the peace.

His hospital, his legacy, is no longer on Pearl's Hill. It had to move twice and is now on Moulmein Road. The modern Tan Tock Seng Hospital is one of the best in the city; every Singaporean knows it and even the country's founder, Lee Kuan Yew was a patient here. But Tan Tock Seng's mortal remains lay buried here on the slope of the hill. Unforgotten and yet almost forgotten.

**Address** 254 Outram Road, Singapore 169051 (Tiong Bahru), on a wooded hill next to the road | **Getting there** MRT to EW 17 Tiong Bahru, then bus 33, 63, 122 or 851 to Eton House Preschool | **Hours** Always accessible | **Tip** The 'airplane houses', former social housing blocks from the 1940s, so called because of their aerodynamic form, are in the hip quarter across the road, Tiong Bahru.

# 98 Tan Yeok Nee's House

*Finding happiness abroad*

If it could talk, the stories this building could tell would fill volumes. In its 125-year history it has been a storehouse for the long-since demolished Cockpit Hotel and served as a school and headquarters of the Salvation Army; a railway official lived here and a business school from Chicago taught here. Today it houses a clinic for Chinese medicine. The pale-yellow building is seen as the only one in Singapore that still demonstrates the architectural style of the Teochew Chinese from the east of Guangzhou.

Its architect, Tan Yeok Nee, wanted to construct a building in the trading centre of Singapore that looked exactly like his own at home in mainland China. It was to embody the balance between yin and yang and present the five elements of fire, water, earth, wood and gold. Tan had to leave his homeland overnight, after betting away the money for his mother's funeral at the card table. In 1844, he reached Southeast Asia with the aim of starting again. In Singapore he first sold textiles at the harbour. Thanks to his friendship with the son of Sultan Ibrahim he was soon vested with the honorary title of Kang-Chu in neighbouring Johor, which secured him special trading rights. Tan's career rocketed from then on. When his friend mounted the throne, he conferred Tan the title of Major China of Johor and appointed him to the council of state. Tan had long since traded in pepper, alcohol and opium and owned his own plantations.

When Tan returned to Singapore as a made man in 1875, he had the title 'Advisor to the Sultan' engraved in Chinese characters above the roof beams of his new house. For the meticulous restoration of the historied memorial in the year 2000, which cost a staggering 12 million Singapore dollars, the architects flew in Teochew craftsmen from China – they could find no one in Singapore who could have carried out the traditional work.

Address 101 Penang Road, Singapore 238466 (Centre) | Getting there MRT to NS 24/NE 6/CC 1 Dhoby Ghaut | Hours Visible only from the outside | Tip The Sri Thendayuthapani Temple (Chettiar's Temple) on Tank Road is one of the most important Hindu temples in the city and the destination of the Thaipusam procession.

# 99_ Tea Chapter

*Slow down like the Queen*

Those who love tea and peace will feel right at home. Here in the soothing, delicately fragranced atmosphere of these rooms, you can really escape the hustle and bustle of Chinatown. Everything about this shophouse, which is furnished like a traditional teahouse, will make you very more than welcome.

Of course it is all about the tea: the lightly fermented Oolong from Fujian is the speciality, and then there's Imperial Golden Cassia. Tea Chapter also sells handpicked varieties on the second floor. Local celebrities have long counted themselves among the shop's clientele, and good taste is only for those who can afford it: 50 grams can cost up to 70 Singapore dollars.

Thirteen tea-lovers founded Tea Chapter in 1989. Their philosophy is to offer all their knowledge about tea and the tea ceremony as well as to sell selected teas. Through this, Tea Chapter has held its position as the biggest teahouse in Singapore to this day. Of course, you can find it all online too. But only here can you smell the teas, try them and experience the real tea culture.

But that's not all there is for sale. Tea Chapter also offers gastronomical specialities to complement its teas, from Dragon Rice Balls and Dim Sum platters to Lychee Tea Jelly – traditional delicacies from China. Best of all, though, is the experience of the centuries-old tea ceremony, which grandmaster Patrick Kang has been celebrating in these halls for more than 20 years. The tea experts also offer workshops and courses for customers, as well as for school classes. These are all about the higher art of preparing every tea in the befitting way. Each tea's complete, wonderful aroma will only develop through the correct interactions.

By the way, Queen Elizabeth II has long appreciated this. The monarch stopped by here for a cuppa during a state visit in 1989, and not for English Breakfast Tea.

Address 9 & 11 Neil Road, Singapore 088808 (Chinatown) | Getting there MRT to EW 16/NE 3 Outram Park | Hours Teahouse Sun–Thu 11am–9pm, Fri & Sat 11am–10.30pm; tea shop Sun–Thu 10.30am–9pm, Fri & Sat 10.30am–10.30pm; book courses at teachapter.com | Tip Feel like something savoury? Walk along to number 120 on the corner of Bukit Pasoh Road, where you will find the street restaurant Chang Shun's must-try roasted chicken rice.

# 100 The Ten Courts of Hell
*Dante's* Inferno *in Chinese*

A guided tour into hell takes place here every Friday evening. Oh, how peaceful Haw Par Villa appeared at first glance...

Those who step through the large Chinese gateway into the theme park will encounter huge plaster figures that radiate a huge variety of colours – Mr Teo's paintbrush has been kept busy to this end for 67 years. His tigers, demons, princesses and warriors stand on the paths that wind up the hill and carry you off into the fantastic world of Chinese myths, imparting the wisdom of life.

But then things start to get serious. A first sign points the way into the 'ten courts of hell'. The second warns against allowing children to enter the hellmouth without being accompanied by their parents. These are flanked by guards, one ox-headed and one horse-faced, who, according to Chinese tradition, drive the souls into the forecourt. Here King Qinguang calls the shots: he separates the good from the bad. The latter then find their way into the inferno. Every imaginable sin and its corresponding punishment is represented here in gaudy colours – scenes that must have haunted many a Singaporean schoolchild. Dante's *Inferno* wouldn't have looked much different and Hieronymus Bosch may have suffered from the same nightmares. But there is an end to the torture: King Zhuanglun sends the tormented to an old lady. She administers the tea of forgetfulness. Now they can be reincarnated.

Aw Boon Haw, who was behind the success of the the herbal ointment Tiger Balm (see ch. 26), was very keen to educate his fellow men. He thought they should deal openly with life, death and reincarnation. He created the park in 1937 to this end. Initially it was a – simply unbelievable – present for his brother Aw Boon Par. He lived at the upper end of the park in a villa with seven rooms. From there he had a view of the open sea, of more than a thousand statues, and of life and death.

Address Haw Par Villa, 262 Pasir Panjang Road, Singapore 118628 (West Coast) | Getting there MRT to CC25 Haw Par Villa | Hours Daily 9am–7pm, guided tours on Friday evenings | Tip In the long-established Manhill Restaurant (99 Pasir Panjang Road) your fellow patrons will mostly be locals – the food is home-style Chinese cooking.

# 101 Thambi Magazine Store
*Singapore's newspaper king*

Sure, there's the Internet. But there is still paper too. And there is Mister Sam. Sam, whose real name is P. Senthilmurugam, runs the Thambi Magazine Store, an El Dorado for all fans of the printed word and image. His kiosk in Holland Village, a lively quarter of wealthy Singaporeans and lots of foreigners, offers more than 4,000 titles from all the corners of the planet, as well as puzzle books, horoscopes and feng shui magazines.

Sam's grandfather came to Singapore as an immigrant, and Sam's father founded the stand at the back of a cinema, on a pasting table under plastic tarp. Sam initially wanted to become a sailor, but grew into the family business, and today he sells his stock along a pavement by a busy junction, the magazines neatly lined up on blue shelves. Sam's brother delivers the daily papers to the surrounding quarters in the middle of the night – from three in the morning he puts together the individual parts, that are brought directly from the printing plant, with his Indian workers. Shortly afterwards Sam drives to his stand and orders the morning papers. 'The arranging of the booklets and newspapers is an art form of its own: you have to really know the different papers to be able to present them correctly.'

The whole family works pretty much around the clock in alternating shifts at the stand, which is also home to a bureau de change. Because his customers often go on long holidays or business trips, they may miss some issues of their favorite magazine or newspaper. No problem: Sam also keeps old issues for a couple of weeks on a floor built in under the roof.

Censorship reigns in Singapore, and sometimes even Sam can't help with certain titles. He has repeatedly had problems with magazines such as Cosmopolitan or Maxim. In minor cases of nakedness on magazine covers though, he simply sticks the price label over the models' nipples – censorship bypassed.

**Address** Corner of 211 Holland Avenue and Lorong Liput, Singapore 258967 (Holland Village) | **Getting there** MRT to CC 21 Holland Village | **Hours** Daily 7am−10pm | **Tip** Thirsty? Cheap, freshly pressed fruit in all possible varieties can be found at 88 Holland Village Fresh Fruit Juice in Holland Village Market & Food Centre diagonally opposite.

# 102___ Thow Kwang Dragon Kiln

*The fire can't be extinguished for ever*

It usually sleeps. Its head down at the bottom, its bulky body stretches and undulates 40 metres up the hill, right at the top is the tip of its tail. Its scales are made of red bricks. This dragon is a kiln, the oldest in Singapore.

It lies dormant in one of the last pieces of jungle. The large dragon kiln, and a little brother next to it, are the last two of at least 10 kilns that were once located here, in a kampong, a village in the middle of the jungle. The soil is very clayey and ideal for pottery. The craft paid off, the kilns were worked to capacity: flowerpots, urns, vases, figures – everything was hand turned. But the opening up of China flooded the market with cheap mass-produced products. That was the end of most of the potteries.

Quality and uniqueness are now once again sought after. This is also thanks to Tan Thow Kwang and his young niece, a master potter, who both wish to preserve the heritage of the 3,000-year-old Chinese tradition of dragon kiln pottery firing. Twice a year they reawaken the dragon. The raw earthenware, most of which is created by artists, is then placed in the five-metre-wide body, while in the head at the front the wood fire is lit and the temperature increased to almost 1,300 degrees. That takes at least 24 hours. The experienced potter recognises the right temperature by the colour of the fire. The door is bricked up, and the heat spreads from the front to the back and escapes out of the tail. The kiln burns for up to a week and then needs just as long to cool down. The state of the pottery can be checked through a side window.

The results are unique: each piece is a one-off, depending on the duration of firing, its location in the kiln and the type of wood used to fire it. This is the reason that many renowned Singaporean and international potters have their objects fired in the old dragon.

**Address** 85 Lorong Tawas, Singapore 639823 (Kranji) | **Getting there** MRT to EW 27 Boon Lay, then bus 199 to Before Lorong Danau | **Hours** Daily 9am – 5pm, bookings at thowkwang.com.sg | **Tip** Trip to the countryside: the Kranji Countryside Express from MRT Kranji will take you to organic farms, goat, frog and koi farms and the Sungei Buloh Wetland Reserve.

# 103___ The Three Samsui Women

*Singapore's Trümmerfrauen*

The little dolls wear red hats and blue suits. They are sold as key rings or fridge magnets. But they actually have a very interesting story to tell, for without the city's *Trümmerfrauen* (German women who helped clear the post-war rubble), Singapore would not be the way it is today. It is for this reason that the Samsui women are also immortalised in many paintings, and the artist Liu Jilin has even dedicated a group of sculptures to them in front of the URA building in Chinatown.

From the 1920s, they came to Singapore from the Samsui district of Guangdong in southern China. During the Great Depression there were too many men looking for work, so the British closed the border to any more. Hard-working women now had the chance to enter the colony. Like most Chinese immigrants, they went to Chinatown. Here they lived in very poor and cramped conditions, mostly among themselves, very often remaining unmarried. The young women were well known for their strong personalities, and they refused to work as prostitutes or in the drug trade.

In fact, they worked on building sites. They carried stones, earth and cement in baskets that hung from both sides of a shoulder yoke, just as they are shown in the sculptures. The distinguishing feature of the female construction workers from Samsui is their red, stiffened and cross-folded cotton hat. It served as protection from the sun and as storage for money and cigarettes, and granted some safety on the building sites. Their blue suits were practical against dirt and dust.

The back-breaking work of these female coolies significantly contributed to the building of Singapore right up to the 1970s. That is why they have entered the collective memory of the city and are publicly revered. This is also why you can now find their souvenirs along with the Merlions and the dragons in the tourist shops.

Address In front of the URA building, 45 Maxwell Road, Singapore 069118 (Chinatown) |
Getting there MRT to EW 15 Tanjong Pagar | Tip In Chinatown Heritage Centre there
are visual representations of life in Chinatown in Singapore's hard early years (tours via
chinatownheritagecentre.com.sg).

# 104__ The Traditional Roaster
*Margarine, sugar and the right bean*

It's a real art form – and the family of the coffee roaster Tan Bong Heong knows how to produce masterpieces, from classic Singaporean *kopi* varieties (see ch. 20) to Western gourmet blends. Their roasting plant on Balestier Road is one of the last family-run companies of its kind in the metropolis. Lam Yeo means, in the Hokkien dialect, 'the southern sea' – just like the Mandarin word '*Nanyang*' that is commonly used in Singapore. Both terms stand for opportunities, hopes and dreams among the Chinese.

The dreams of the Tans have been realised. Their roasting plant has been housed in the same shophouse since 1959, and not much has changed there since those beginnings. The teak shelves, full of old coffee cups, cans and barrels, in which coffee beans were stored, still line the walls to the ceiling. In the middle of the room is the two-storey-tall counter, with coffee containers from the 1950s filled with 10 different varieties of coffee bean. The signature blend is ground using the best South Asian beans in the two grinders here. The whole thing feels like an old-fashioned pharmacy or sweetshop.

The most popular varieties among locals are still the *kopis* (see ch. 20), which are served in the local coffee shops and the hawker stalls in the markets. The beans are roasted with sugar and margarine, giving *kopi* its wonderful, slightly caramelised flavour. Whether drunk with or without sugar, with condensed milk or black or with ice, this typical Singaporean flavour always comes through. Nowadays even decaffeinated coffee is roasted by him.

Singaporeans love coffee, and so now there is also a coffee trade fair. But Lam Yeo stays true to itself: the family only wants to roast coffee, nothing more and nothing less. Tan explains that his secret is down to selecting the best beans. He knows how best to roast them and has a feeling for the ideal blend, and this is something his customers have valued for decades.

Address Lam Yeo Coffee Powder Factory, 328 Balestier Road, Singapore 329760
(Balestier) | Getting there MRT to NS 20 Novena, then bus 21, 124, 130, 131 or 145 to
After Pegu Road | Hours Mon – Sat 9am – 5pm | Tip At Boon Tong Kee, a little further
along the road at number 399, you will find classic Chinese-Singaporean specialities such
as Hainanese chicken rice.

# 105__ The URA

*A model of the city of the future*

URA is the abbreviation for Urban Redevelopment Authority. This makes it sound very much like a boring governmental office and therefore not necessarily worthy of a visit.

But here in Singapore you'd be really missing out on something – they make plans not only for a city, but for a state too. All of this becomes apparent on a visit: a miniature model that illustrates, to anyone who wants to know, what the future of the tropical island will look like, stretches over two storeys of the URA.

Urban planning in Singapore follows a masterplan that was already put together in 1958. Since 1998 it has been reconsidered and adjusted every five years – Singapore's development is more rapid than in almost any other city in the world. The little red dot, as Singapore likes to call itself, needs constant development to be able to survive. Without any natural resources, the island is always searching for new ideas. And the URA is the mastermind: land use, construction development plans, preservation orders, infrastructure projects – this is the interface between environmental sustainability and economic development. Parking spaces and public parks are designated, water reservoirs created, islands and land extended and reclaimed and subterranean living spaces conceived.

Exhibitions explain the city's big issues, such as its provision of water and energy. A model workshop decorates the huge wooden panels in lovingly detailed work. The miniature city on them grows year by year. In this way you can comprehend the current portfolio and the projects of the future at any given time. You can literally see how Marina Bay is to be built up further. Or where the future harbour will be located. But you can also see how Raffles laid out the various quarters, how the Singapore River and its tributaries have decisively influenced land development. And how green the city actually is.

**Address** 45 Maxwell Road, Singapore 069118 (Chinatown) | **Getting there** MRT to EW 15 Tanjong Pagar | **Hours** Mon – Sat 9am–5pm | **Tip** The Maxwell Food Centre, one of the city's most popular and best hawker centres, is right outside the door.

# 106___ The Vertical Garden

*The jungle climbs up the building*

Nature in Singapore is more than just trees and bushes. It is a capital good. The self-chosen promotional slogan has long been the city's programme: the 'Garden City' of the 1970s became the 'City in the Garden' of the 2000s – more compact, more modern, but always green. Because green is an economic factor and a competitive edge in Singapore. But how can a rapidly growing city maintain its greenery and even increase it? The island's cultivable land is becoming ever more scarce, street planting in the inner city is at its limit. All that remains is to look upwards.

The trend of vertical vegetation comes from France. While its prominent representatives, the architect Jean Nouvel and the botanist Patrick Blanc, often struggle with the mere preservation of the vegetation in European latitudes, the ideal conditions to successfully create green walls prevail in Singapore thanks to its tropical climate. But even here near the equator the greenery needs sophisticated, unseen technology. The Living Green Facades are made up of local plants and are provided with water by an automatic irrigation system. They often also grow as hydroponics. Skyscrapers in green coats, like the Oasia Hotel tower on the border to Chinatown, are created in this way. Here gardens on several floors create the impression of a vertical oasis. And we wouldn't be in Singapore if the greenery didn't pay off: dust, noise and sunlight are filtered, buildings need much less air-conditioning and thus save on energy and money. But above all, the equatorial island has recognised that cities that are good to live in attract investors, workforces and tourists.

This is why Singapore is so proud of its tropical-engineered green city landscape. If bamboo was hitherto seen as the symbol of Asian strength, it has been overgrown in the meantime by the never withering green of the facades: it represents the adaptability of a dynamic society.

Address Oasia Hotel, 100 Peck Seah Street, Singapore 079333 (Chinatown) | Getting there MRT to EW15 Tanjog Pagar | Hours Hotel opening hours | Tip The Tippling Club at 38 Tanjong Pagar Road, with its restaurant and bar, was officially one of the 50 best bars in Asia in 2017.

# 107 __ The Victoria Theatre

*Throw it away? No chance!*

An old lady is given a facelift, make-up applied and hair dressed. And behold: she radiates in resplendent beauty. In this way she becomes a symbol for Singapore's newly discovered appreciation of the old and handed-down. The Victoria Theatre and Concert Hall is a jewel in any case. It is in fact two jewels, which were joined together at a later date: the Victoria Theatre, the city's oldest stage, completed in 1862 (when it was originally Singapore's Town Hall), and the concert hall from the year 1905. The duo have long slumbered in a deep sleep, even though they are located at the city's top address, at the mouth of the Singapore River.

But it was as if the stage and concert hall were just waiting to be revived. It cost a trifling 158 million Singapore dollars and took several years. But in 2014 the unexpected came to pass. The two old buildings had become the most modern art institute in the city. More important still: the planners from W architects used as much of the pre-existent building materials as possible. The foyer was sound insulated by mounting the three-centimetre-thick back-rests of the former theatre seats on the walls. The cast iron fittings of the chairs now lead a second life as holders of the wooden wall panels in the concert hall. And the former side parts support the new railings.

With this the architects established a trend – this ultra-modern city had previously tended to throw away anything that became outdated. Recycling? A big zero. But the Victoria has shown how it is done. An example is the clock in its tower. It was only completed in 1906, one year after the opening of the building. The clock with its diameter of four metres cost 6,000 Straits dollars at the time – today that would be a good two million. Its English builders renovated it in 2012. Some things just take a bit longer at Victoria Theatre. But it's always worth the wait.

Address 9 Empress Place, Singapore 179556 (Colonial District) | Getting there MRT to EW 13/NS 25 City Hall | Hours Daily 10am–9pm | Tip On the free-to-access roof terrace of the National Gallery Singapore (1 St Andrew's Road), there are two lounges with fantastic views of the skyline, open in the afternoon with drinks and small dishes.

# 108___Wan Qing Yuan
*The revolutionary in the villa*

Teo Eng Hock had actually bought this villa, whose airy style wasn't uncommon in British Singapore, in 1905 as a retirement home for his mother. Today the spacious house has become a protected monument for its now rare architectural style. But it became famous because of its permanent guest at the start of the 20th century, the Chinese republican Sun Yat Sen. Today the villa is a museum for the close connection between the revolutionary and the Nanyang region.

Sun met Teo Eng Hock in the summer of 1905 on a trip from Japan to Europe. Won over by Sun's idea of driving out the Qing emperor and proclaiming a republic in China, Teo got his mother's permission to accommodate the thinker as their guest. It would appear that Sun liked the spacious house, as in 1906 he founded the Singaporean arm of Tongmenghui, the Chinese Revolutionary Alliance, here. Wan Qing Yuan, as the house has been called to this day, became the seat of the subversives. From here they managed the three uprisings in 1907 and 1908. And this is where Sun designed the flag from the Republic of China, which Teo's wife then sewed together in the evenings. Ultimately the rebels around Sun Yat Sen managed to expel the hated emperor of China in 1911.

Teo sold the house in 1910. Wealthy Chinese transferred it to the Chinese Chamber of Commerce in 1938. The government of the Chinese Republic contributed to transforming it into a museum for Sun's movement. But it actually went through various other hands before it found its ultimate destiny: on the 100th anniversary of the Chinese Revolution of 1911, the office of monuments opened the memorial.

In the garden there are two bronze statues of the erstwhile leader of the Chinese, who is now venerated in Taiwan – one sitting and one standing with swaying coattails, as if he were thinking about the future of his homeland.

晚晴园

这座英雄别墅始建于时时的历史建筑，为晚清侨商张永福于1902年所建。1905年，张永福将此墅赠置别业作为"晚晴园"，供奉佛者。同年，孙中山麻那初访新，张永福捐供此别墅作为中山信馆，从此晚晴园成为同盟会南洋总革命基地。

辛亥革命前夕，孙中山访问新加坡七次，其中四次住在晚晴园。孙中山在晚晴园成立中国同盟会总部加坡分会。起草联合盟会组章。设立策源支部，存放所用的临次（1907年5月），《民报》南版次（1907年12月期间同盟会成立次（1908年4月）。

Address Sun Yat Sen Nanyang Memorial Hall, 12 Tai Gin Road, Singapore 327874 (Toa Payoh) | Getting there MRT to NS 19 Toa Payoh, then three stations with bus 139 or 145 to Zhongshan Mall | Hours Tue–Sun 10am–5pm, guided tours at sysnmh.org.sg | Tip The Buddhist Lian Shan Shuang Lin Monastery (184 Jalan Toa Payoh) is a very spacious, beautiful site with a temple and seven-storey pagoda.

# 109_Whampoa Dragon Fountain

*Tell me where the dragons are...*

There's one here still. Upright, head stretched towards the sky, mouth wide open, elongating his powerful body with clawed front and back feet, as if he were about to take off. The moment of movement is so realistically represented you almost wish he would. But this dragon is a fountain figure, his colourful scales are made of broken porcelain, and he stands bound to a pedestal in front of a residential block.

In the past there were many of these figures on the island. Very few have escaped the rapid urban development. And even this one has seen much better days, as the older residents complain. Back then the sculpture was illuminated and there was water in the fountain. All that is long gone.

At the same time, the dragon is the symbol for strength and power in Asia, and is the most powerful animal of all in feng shui teaching. It is deeply rooted in the Asian culture and many Singaporeans believe in its mythical powers. According to feng shui understanding, the whole of Singapore is dragon country. Five dragons wind imaginarily through the island, one central and four more, one for each point of the compass. Each dragon is distinguished by a characteristic, an element and a colour. The island's most important dragons are the central and the southern ones, standing for wealth and prosperity. Business is particularly successful along their bodies, for example on Orchard Road. But the areas around the head possess the greatest energy: Fort Canning Hill, Mount Emily, Pearl's Hill, to name but a few. The financial district of Marina Bay is located within the sphere of influence of three heads at once and therefore possesses very bright development potential.

Whampoa residents want to keep their dragon as a contemporary witness. But its future can be far from safe when even the five-dragon fountain at the foot of Fort Canning Hill has already been pulled down.

Address In front of Block 85 on Whampoa Drive, Singapore 320085 (Whampoa) |
Getting there MRT to NE 9 Boon Keng, then by taxi | Tip Walking back along the
road towards Balestier Road you will come across Sing Hon Loong, one of only a few
typical toast bread bakeries left here.

# 110 Ying Fo Fui Clan House
*A home abroad*

Singapore, the city of immigrants: practically none of those who lived here at the foundation of the city in 1819 saw it as their home. But all of them saw a chance to earn money quickly here. That's why they stayed. Homesickness prevailed. The Tamils, often used as slave labourers by the British, longed to be back in the sun of southern India. And the Chinese, some of them coolies, but many soon wealthy businesspeople, wanted at least to be buried in the village of their births in mainland China. They all dreamed of returning home.

In order to facilitate their start in the foreign city and to keep them on board, the clan houses emerged. Hokkien, Teochew, Cantonese or Hakka could hardly understand one another – their mother tongues were too different. This was another reason that they all created a piece of home abroad.

The first clan group is said to have been founded by Tsao Ah Chih, the chef of the city's founder Sir Stamford Raffles, back in the year of arrival 1819. Eighty years later the growing city already had more than 50 clan clubs, and by now it is said to be a good 200. The members helped each other, festivals were celebrated together, some built their own temples and ultimately the clan even took care of the repatriation of a member's bones to China, a bit like an insurance policy. Members also collected millions of dollars for the defence of China against the Japanese invasion.

An example of one of the numerous clan houses in Chinatown is Ying Fo Fui, the first Hakka Chinese club in Singapore. They established their club in 1822, and built their house in 1844. To this day it has only one doorway and no windows – in this way it reflects traditional Hakka villages, which were fortified by outer walls. But the house also symbolises the closed society, to which outsiders have no admission. And is therefore a place of rest, and yearning.

Address 98 Telok Ayer Street, Singapore 048474 (Chinatown) | Getting there MRT to DT 18 Telok Ayer | Hours Mon–Sat 9am–5pm, Sun 11am–5pm | Tip The picturesque Taoist Thian Hock Keng Temple at 158 Telok Ayer Street has been carefully restored and is once again resplendent in its original colours and masterly craftsmanship.

# 111_ Youth Olympic Park

*Faded memories of young athletes*

The palm trees look slightly bashful, as if they had been stood up. But in fact the three neat rows recollect a mega event for Singapore. The city state was the first organiser of the Youth Olympic Games, in August 2010. Every Olympic committee of the countries participating received a palm tree – Germany's is in the first row, second from the right, at the fountain in front of Marina Bay Sands.

The palm trees are only part of the installation that commemorates the games. If you cross the Helix bridge you will find the small, almost forgotten Youth Olympic Park. Artworks by Singaporean youths contributed to its design. The centrepiece of the remnants of the games is the huge raft that floats out in front of the grandstand: the games' opening and closing events took place on the largest floating stage in the world in front of the 25,000-seater stand, which has since been used for numerous other large-scale events – such as the annual National Day Parade.

The games were at least as controversial in Singapore as the globally admired Formula One night race the city state has hosted at great cost since 2008. However, the mood in those weeks in the summer of 2010 was fantastic – Singapore showed itself to be cosmopolitan, thousands of volunteers offered advice and support, and more than 3,500 young athletes became ambassadors for the island. But the population bemoaned that many of the stadia were only half full, and some complained as vehemently as is allowed in Singapore that the whole thing was firstly senseless because it did nothing for the city, and secondly was much too expensive.

That is of course nonsense. Thanks to the pictures on television, Singapore managed to polish its reputation – from a boring 'fine city' to a fun modern metropolis. That is certainly worth its weight in gold. The signs under the palm trees may already be largely faded, but the effect that they triggered persists.

Address Raffles Avenue at the Helix Bridge and along Marina Bay Promenade in front of Marina Bay Sands, 018956 (Marina Bay) | Getting there MRT to CE1/DT16 Bayfront | Tip Only the best international design is brought together in the Red Dot Design Museum in the pavilion to the right of Marina Bay Sands. Many award-winning pieces can be bought in the museum shop.

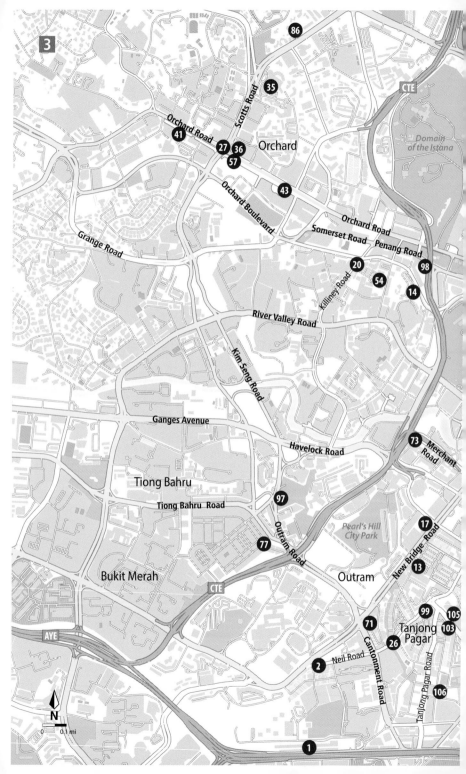

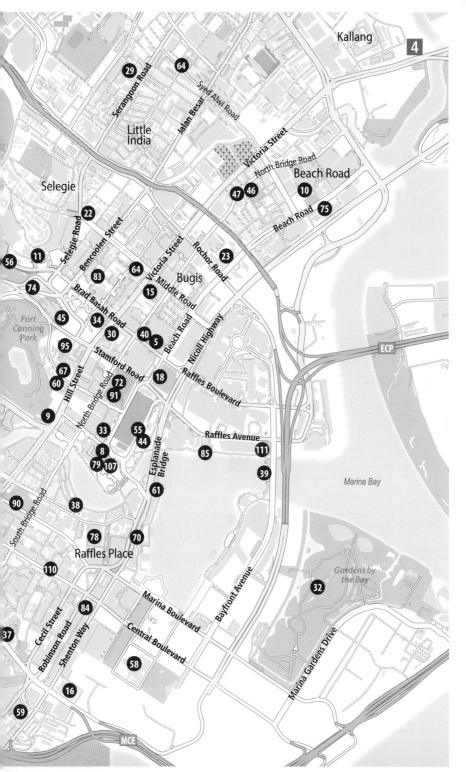

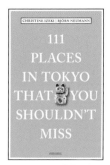

Christine Izeki, Björn Neumann
**111 Places in Tokyo**
**That You Shouldn't Miss**
ISBN 978-3-7408-0024-6

Kathrin Bielfeldt, Raymond Wong,
Jürgen Bürger
**111 Places in Hong Kong**
**That You Shouldn't Miss**
ISBN 978-3-95451-936-1

Sharon Fernandes
**111 Places In New Delhi**
**That You Must Not Miss**
ISBN 978-3-95451-648-3

Marcus X. Schmid
**111 Places in Istanbul**
**That You Must Not Miss**
ISBN 978-3-95451-423-6

Lucia Jay von Seldeneck,
Carolin Huder
**111 Places in Berlin**
**That You Shouldn't Miss**
ISBN 978-3-95451-208-9

Alexia Amvrazi, Diana Farr Louis,
Diane Shugart
**111 Places in Athens**
**That You Shouldn't Miss**
ISBN 978-3-7408-0377-3

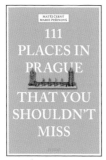

Matěj Černý, Marie Peřinová
**111 Places in Prague**
**That You Shouldn't Miss**
ISBN 978-3-7408-0144-1

Andrea Livnat, Angelika Baumgartner
**111 Places in Tel Aviv**
**That You Shouldn't Miss**
ISBN 978-3-7408-0263-9

Jo-Anne Elikann
**111 Places in New York**
**That You Must Not Miss**
ISBN 978-3-95451-052-8

Laszlo Trankovits, Rüdiger Liedtke
**111 Places in Cape Town**
**That You Must Not Miss**
ISBN 978-3-95451-610-0

Amy Bizzarri, Susie Inverso
**111 Places in Chicago**
**That You Must Not Miss**
ISBN 978-3-7408-0156-4

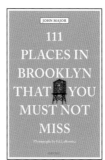

John Major, Ed Lefkowicz
**111 Places in Brooklyn**
**That You Must Not Miss**
ISBN 978-3-7408-0380-3

Anita Mai Genua, Clare Davenport,
Elizabeth Lenell Davies
**111 Places in Toronto That You
Must Not Miss**
ISBN 978-3-7408-0257-8

Benjamin Haas, Leonie Friedrich
**111 Places in Buenos Aires
That You Must Not Miss**
ISBN 978-3-7408-0260-8

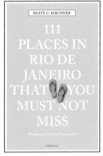

Beate C. Kirchner
**111 Places in Rio de Janeiro
That You Must Not Miss**
ISBN 978-3-7408-0262-2

Andréa Seiger
**111 Places in Washington D.C.
That You Must Not Miss**
ISBN 978-3-7408-0258-5

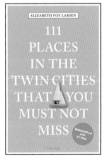

Elisabeth Larsen
**111 Places in The Twin Cities
That You Must Not Miss**
ISBN 978-3-7408-0029-1

Joe DiStefano, Clay Williams
**111 Places in Queens
That You Must Not Miss**
ISBN 978-3-7408-0020-8

Allison Robicelli, John Dean
**111 Places in Baltimore**
**That You Must Not Miss**
ISBN 978-3-7408-0158-8

Laurel Moglen, Julia Posey,
Lyudmila Zotova
**111 Places in Los Angeles**
**That You Must Not Miss**
ISBN 978-3-95451-884-5

Gordon Streisand
**111 Places in Miami and the**
**Keys That You Must Not Miss**
ISBN 978-3-95451-644-5

Floriana Petersen, Steve Werney
**111 Places in San Francisco**
**That You Must Not Miss**
ISBN 978-3-95451-609-4

John Sykes, Birgit Weber
**111 Places in London**
**That You Shouldn't Miss**
ISBN 978-3-95451-346-8

Tom Shields, Gillian Tait
**111 Places Glasgow**
**That You Shouldn't Miss**
ISBN 978-3-7408-0256-1

**Dr Christoph Hein** has lived in Singapore, where he works as a correspondent for a newspaper, for 20 years. He loves wandering through the city with his wife Sabine, deciphering its many secrets bit by bit. This is a laborious task – but one they are dedicated to, if they don't happen to be travelling the rest of Asia with their daughter or enjoying the cold rain of their native Germany.

**Sabine Hein-Seppeler** has lived in Singapore with her husband Christoph for 20 years. The travel book author and newspaper correspondent have long since taken the 'little red dot', as Singapore refers to its own place on the map, with the friendliness of its people and the diversity of their cultures, into their hearts. They love wandering through the city, deciphering its many secrets bit by bit. This is a laborious task – but one they are dedicated to, if they don't happen to be travelling the rest of Asia with their daughter or enjoying the cold rain of their native Germany.